Bariatric Bombshell

An Honest Approach to Weight Loss Surgery Success

STEPHANIE SEHESTEDT

Copyright © 2023 by Stephanie Sehestedt

All rights reserved.

No portion of this book may be reproduced in any form without written permission from the publisher or author, except as permitted by U.S. copyright law.

Although the author and publisher have made every effort to ensure that the information in this book was correct at press time, the author and publisher do not assume and hereby disclaim any liability to any party for any loss, damage, or disruption caused by errors or omissions, whether such errors or omissions result from negligence, accident, or any other cause.

Some of the names and details used to portray real-life stories in this book have been changed to protect the identity of the individuals in them. In the case that an individual's real name has been used, written permission has been provided by the individual.

Adherence to all applicable laws and regulations, including international, federal, state, and local governing professional licensing, business practices, advertising, and all other aspects of doing business in the US, Canada, or any other jurisdiction, is the sole responsibility of the reader and consumer.

Neither the author nor the publisher assumes any responsibility or liability whatsoever on behalf of the consumer or reader of this material. Any perceived slight of any individual or organization is purely unintentional.

The resources in this book are provided for informational purposes only and should not be used for diagnosis and/or treatment. Please consult your medical professional before making changes to your diet, exercise routine, medical regimen, lifestyle, and/or mental health care.

Neither the author nor the publisher can be held responsible for the use of the information provided within this book. Please always consult a trained professional before making any decision regarding the treatment of yourself or others.

For more information, email stephanie@bariatricbombshell.com.

ISBN 978-1-962133-40-1

PLATYPUS
PUBLISHING

To Kelsey and all of my incredible patients, I am inspired by your grace and strength as I witness your hard-won transformations. Thank you for letting me in, trusting me, and allowing me to guide you. Knowing you is a blessing, and my life is changed as yours is!

CONTENTS

INTRODUCTION	IX
Part 1: CLARITY	1
1. The Big Realization	3
2. Shake It Off: Seven Misconceptions	11
3. Advice from Bariatric Care Providers	21
Part 2: DIRECTION	31
4. Timing Is Everything: How to Qualify	33
5. Insurance Pebbles: Roll with It	41
6. Talking to Your Doctors & Choosing Your Surgeon	47
7. Mapping It Out: The Bariatric Process	53
Part 3: INSPIRATION	63
8. Find Your Why	65
9. Create Your Success Mindset	71
Part 4: ACTION	81
10. Start Now, Here's How	83
11. Making It Last	99
12. Guidelines that Seem Simple yet Are Incredibly Important	107
13. Wisdom from Bariatric Patients	113
Part 5: EMPOWERMENT	125
14. Focus on the Outcome	127
15. Progress Equals Happiness	131
RESOURCES	137
Six Steps for Lasting Behavior Change	138

Family-Friendly Habits to Start Now	139
Your Bombshell Action Plan	140
What to Say When Calling Your Insurance Company	144
The Bariatric Pantry & Refrigerator	145
Meal & Snack Ideas	152
Family-Friendly Recipes & How to Modify Your Own	161
Holiday & Dining Out Tips	168
Evidence-Based Diet Plans for Healthy Eating Ideas*	170
Your Anytime, Anywhere Guide to Being Active	171
Recommended Reading	174
ACKNOWLEDGMENTS	177
PERMISSIONS	179
NOTES	180

INTRODUCTION

Have you ever considered the difference between success and failure? Or that success is often born from failure or adversity? Many of us know someone who has had weight loss surgery. Some are enjoying better health and quality of life. Unfortunately, others have ended up right back where they started. So what's the difference?

In this book, I want to share what I have observed and learned as a bariatric nurse, clinical coordinator, and health coach. It has been my privilege for over fifteen years to accompany individuals on a personal level throughout their weight loss journeys.

This book is a culmination of my **experiences, interactions** with patients, and my **unwavering belief in the potential for transformation**. Through these pages, I share insights gained from countless one-on-one appointments with weight loss patients, helping them qualify for weight loss surgery and find success thereafter.

We will explore **evidence-based strategies** for long-term weight loss surgery success. You will gain a new perspective as we unravel the common misconceptions, learn how to build **family-friendly habits** that support the bariatric lifestyle, and read **real-life stories** and remarks from weight loss surgery patients who want to share what they have learned. To give you a head start, I even offer advice directly to you from bariatric team members.

The bariatric path is profound and intricate. It requires honesty with yourself, an incredible level of support, and dedication. However, for those who choose this direction, it can lead to remarkable improvements in quality of life and overall wellness. This book aims to **offer guidance and encouragement**, helping to alleviate some of the challenges that patients and their loved ones may encounter throughout the pre- and postoperative phases.

Whether you are considering weight loss surgery for yourself or supporting someone you love, you'll find that this book is a valuable resource designed to provide practical advice. Together, we will navigate the complexities of bariatric surgery. We will also explore the power of self-monitoring and embracing a positive mindset, fashioning the cornerstone of your bariatric knowledge foundation as you shed old ways of thinking and open yourself to limitless possibilities.

Even so, this book is not intended to be a comprehensive guide to weight loss surgery. There are some excellent books with that purpose, which I recommend in the resources section, along with additional helpful reading. I also want to emphasize that the advice provided in this book should not replace the medical guidance of your healthcare team. They are there to guide, direct, and care for you as you endeavor to enjoy better health.

Please use this book however it is most helpful. Skip around and take what you need. It will be a valuable resource you can turn to again and again for guidance and inspiration.

I have written specifically to those considering weight loss surgery, but anyone seeking a better understanding of what's involved can benefit from the contents herein.

This book consists of five parts:

1. **Clarity**, where you will eliminate misconceptions and gain a head start with helpful advice from bariatric team members.
2. **Direction**, where we will break down the process of qualifying and preparing for bariatric surgery.
3. **Inspiration**, where we will focus on mindset shifts to help create lasting change, leading to weight loss surgery success.
4. **Action**, which includes detailed guidance on how to start implementing healthy habits and how they will benefit you.
5. **Empowerment**, where we will discuss the importance of positivity and focusing on the outcome you desire from your long-term goals.

INTRODUCTION

In the resources section, I have included many of my quick guides, such as meal and exercise ideas, that patients and providers most commonly ask me for.

It is never too late to start making small changes that can lead to immeasurable progress. While I can't guarantee that you will have the perfect weight loss journey, I can promise you that the information in this book will help you understand what to expect during the bariatric process and how to succeed with long-term surgical weight loss.

As you become armed with new knowledge, you will see that this book is not just about weight loss surgery—**it's about reclaiming your life and rediscovering your passions**. It's about the mindset shifts that have helped me and countless others break free from the shackles of self-doubt and reclaim our vitality. It's about recognizing your inner worthiness of love, success, and happiness.

In the face of a growing obesity epidemic, we must explore and utilize **all avenues toward improved health**. Let us pave the road to understanding, support, and empowerment as we strive to build better lives, promoting wellness in ourselves, our families, and our communities.

Part I: CLARITY

Any surgical procedure carries its set of questions and concerns: What are the risks versus the benefits? What are the possible complications that may arise? How do I prevent them? What about recovery time? How much pain will there be? How will I tolerate it? Add in the many ways your life will change because you are having a weight loss procedure that will affect you for the rest of your life—it's a lot.

These are all questions that your bariatric surgeon will address with you. Of course, **the goal is to achieve a positive surgical outcome**, which means you and your surgeon are both happy with your results. You, as the patient, can assist your surgeon and healthcare team in creating that positive outcome. You'll need to consider the many points covered in this book before surgery. Doing so lets you focus more on the specific instructions for each phase of surgery.

This section focuses on clearing up some common misconceptions about weight loss surgery, including my own previous misunderstanding. **A realistic sense of what bariatric surgery entails will guide you in your decision-making**. This information took me decades to learn, so I hope to save you some trouble by sharing it now. As I present the experience that has elevated my understanding of weight loss surgery, I hope you will embrace your own adventure as you set out on the road toward better health and heightened knowledge.

What's more, I do not approach these topics lightly, as some may trigger intense feelings. If this happens, please know that I never intend to hurt or offend you. But please acknowledge those feelings as a signal that it may be time to seek additional support and direction from a behavioral counselor. I say this with love. Please don't ignore your feelings; don't push them away. Now is the time to talk to someone and gain personalized guidance to ensure success.

I recently had a patient in a support group share that four years after surgery and working with her counselor, she now realizes some of the patterns she still needs to work on to prevent falling back into old habits. That realization came from a woman who has excelled in achieving her weight loss goal, improving her health, and keeping the weight off. She was surprised at how easy it is for old thoughts and habits to come back after weight loss surgery success. And she stressed the importance of working with a counselor who can help with self-awareness.

We ALL can benefit from a mental health counselor to help us keep things in perspective as we navigate life's challenges. As I tell my patients, **long-term weight loss is much more mental than physical**. Most of it starts and stops with what is happening inside our minds.

Weight loss surgery is a serious and complex topic. As much as I have tried to make reading this book enjoyable and valuable, I treat it with great responsibility that you have chosen to invest your time, money, energy, and thought in allowing me to guide you.

Before we begin, I also recommend that you gain as many perspectives as possible before surgery by exploring different resources and talking to people who have had bariatric surgery. As you continue to research, you will read and hear the good, the bad, and the ugly. That is good! But please know that **no surgical weight loss journey is just like another**. You are unique, and so is your path. The best thing you can do is **trust and follow the instructions and guidance that *your* surgeon provides for *you***. Let's start building your knowledge foundation by unraveling some myths and creating a new outlook.

Chapter 1

The Big Realization

If you don't like something, change it. If you can't change it, change your attitude.
— Maya Angelou

Janet puffed, half-heartedly walking one last lap with me. As we rounded the corner through the outer halls of the arena, her words hit me like a bombshell. She confided in me, her voice filled with exhaustion and vulnerability, "I'm considering weight loss surgery." Shock and disappointment washed over me.

"Oh, Janet," I exclaimed, my voice tinged with concern. "You don't need surgery to achieve your goals. I know you can do this. Look at the progress you've already made."

But Janet's tired eyes and the sweat dripping down her face told a different story.

"I still have over a hundred pounds to lose," she declared, with a tone that expressed the depth of her worries, "and I'm concerned about my health."

We had been working together toward her fitness goals for almost four months, as I finished my internship for my degree in exercise science and nutrition. I hated that our time together would soon end, and I longed to see her through to the finish line. She was such a kind and intelligent woman. Yet, in the process of having kids and giving her all to her family and career, she had lost her grip on her physical health and gained significant weight.

Janet's words echoed in my head like they were echoing across the massive halls we walked. I gazed through glass trophy cases as we trudged past them through the empty corridor. Rays of sunshine poured in from the windows above, drawing my eyes to the century-old team photos, gleaming trophies, and bronzed basketballs. The history and spirit of the coaches and players seemed to radiate from the displays. I longed to somehow transfer their energy and enthusiasm to Janet. However, no amount of determination would help her reach her goal without some additional tools. Deep down, Janet knew she needed weight loss surgery as one of those tools.

REGRET

Twenty years later, reflecting on that moment, I wish I could find Janet, look her in the eyes, and apologize for my judgment. Where were my compassion and open-mindedness? What she deserved from me as her instructor was unwavering support and encouragement, not criticism. She had genuinely tried everything in her power to lose the weight and finally faced a difficult decision.

I had failed to recognize the depth of Janet's struggle with obesity and the courage it took for her to open up. I would now happily proclaim that bariatric surgery can be invaluable for achieving long-term weight loss. I would commend her bravery for considering it.

I wish I had told Janet that I believed in her wholeheartedly and assured her that her journey was not one she had to face alone. But I didn't know then what I know now. My previous bias, which regarded weight loss surgery as the easy way out, couldn't have been further from the truth.

THE TRUTH

Bariatric medicine encompasses the study, causes, treatment, and prevention of obesity. Within this field, bariatric surgery has emerged as a time-tested solution. Procedures like the gastric sleeve and bypass, when combined with behavioral and lifestyle modifications, have consistently demonstrated their ability to facilitate lasting weight loss and improve overall health.[1]

Between 2011 and 2021, an estimated 2.3 million people had a surgical weight loss procedure in the US.[2] That figure does not account for the thousands of people who opted to travel to Mexico or other countries, paying out of pocket for their surgeries due to insurance coverage limitations. The number of surgeries performed has increased annually, with the exception of 2020, when surgical procedures were restricted during the COVID-19 pandemic.

The growing popularity of these procedures stems from one simple fact: they work. Countless lives have transformed as patients diligently adopt new habits and embrace the bariatric lifestyle. Yet, despite their remarkable achievements, patients still face disapproving glances and cutting remarks from those who mistakenly believe they should have done it "the hard way."

Nothing is easy about having weight loss surgery. Patients undergo a rigorous evaluation process, including consultations with medical professionals, nutritionists, and mental health experts. They commit to significantly changing their eating habits, physical activity levels, and overall lifestyle, such as quitting smoking. Patients follow strict guidelines for weeks at a time pre- and postoperatively. Weight loss surgery is not a shortcut—it is a tool that empowers individuals to reclaim their health and well-being.

MY STORY

You may be thinking, "Who is this nurse who thinks she can write a book about this stuff?" Let me share my story.

Looking back on myself—as that new graduate, obnoxious with newfound knowledge and the confidence that comes with a university degree, **I had so much to learn.** I thought my education and experience in diet, exercise, and natural health were sufficient to live my passion for helping others to be healthy. I was determined to positively affect lives.

While in college, I also studied under a naturopathic doctor and managed her nutrition store. I provided personal training in multiple fitness facilities. During my university studies, I worked as a child nutrition specialist for a large school district. Then, after graduating, I received additional training as a professional weight loss counselor.

However, none of those experiences gave me an understanding of the deep anguish that many suffering from obesity endure. I had yet to comprehend the emotional and physical struggles. The shame, the self-doubt, and the daily battles with food and self-image were so much deeper than my current understanding.

At twenty-nine, after holding so many different professional roles, I knew I needed a better platform to help others enjoy better health. I wasn't reaching enough people on the level I knew I could. I wanted to inspire and guide people like Janet who are ready to transform their lives. That platform to better reach individuals would come from bariatric nursing.

The tragic loss of my dear friend, Garnett, at the young age of forty-five due to diabetes and its devastating effects weighed heavily on my heart. Living next door to her, I watched her slowly decline as a small sore on her foot led to an amputation. She had gotten it from walking barefoot in her yard; it had become infected and would not heal despite ongoing treatment.

She had to start dialysis shortly after that and struggled to follow her diet and blood glucose management regimen. Unfortunately, despite all treatment efforts, her kidneys failed, and she required a kidney transplant. She heartbreakingly battled illness while taking her immunosuppressant medications, which kept her body from rejecting the new kidney. Several months later, she died while fighting pneumonia.

Losing a friend like Garnett that way was hard to wrap my head around, and I yearned to find a way to prevent others from experiencing the same fate. With a sense of purpose and determination, I started nursing school, unsure of where it would ultimately lead me.

Nursing became my driving force, a means to make a difference in the lives of those affected by obesity and its related health conditions, like type 2 diabetes. Little did I know that this decision would open doors to a world of compassion, understanding, and the opportunity to provide holistic care and guidance to individuals grasping for better health.

Upon completing my nursing degree with top honors, I eagerly dove into the field of medical/surgical nursing. Working in our local hospital's bustling med/surg department, I lovingly and thoughtfully cared for sick and postoperative patients. While I knew that specializing was in my future, I remained uncertain about which path to pursue. There were many opportunities to

THE BIG REALIZATION

discuss healthy lifestyle habits with patients, but ultimately, that wasn't why they were there. They were there to heal and recover.

Everything clicked into place during a hospital training session on the newly established bariatric program. I knew I had to be a part of this transformative field. I possessed a wealth of knowledge and expertise that could profoundly impact individuals seeking weight loss. So, I anxiously approached the clinical coordinator after the training.

A few weeks later, I sat in the boardroom with the entire bariatric team and hospital administrators as our new surgeon reviewed my resume. He smirked a little as he cracked a joke about everyone getting their start at McDonald's (Ironically, I did work there when I was fifteen, but I was old enough at this point that it wasn't on my resume anymore, phew!). Slowly, his eyebrows raised in an expression of surprise and approval. He was impressed, and I was in.

Despite my lingering belief that surgery was not the ultimate solution, I was determined to help patients on their weight loss journeys by teaching them everything I knew about weight loss. I dove in head-first, got organized, and started doing what I love most—counseling patients. I educated them, helped them set goals, created personalized meal and workout plans, and helped them track their progress as they worked toward surgery.

What struck me early on while teaching surgical and non-surgical patients healthy habits was the realization that, **for some individuals**, weight struggles and health issues persist despite their best efforts—**no matter how diligently they adhere to dietary guidelines, engage in physical activity, or follow medical advice, controlling their weight remains a constant battle**. They find themselves burdened with health problems, reliant on handfuls of medications, and unable to participate in activities they once enjoyed.

As we explored the various aspects of their weight struggles—physiological, psychological, environmental, social, spiritual, or financial—it became increasingly evident that for many of these patients, the non-modifiable factors outweighed the modifiable ones. They faced significant barriers that hindered their progress. It became apparent to me that they *needed* the additional tool of bariatric surgery to help transform their lives. This sobering truth served as a clear reminder of the complexity of obesity and the personal challenges faced by each individual.

It was mind-blowing to me. Instead of continuing to torture these patients with piles of educational pamphlets, meal plans, and exercise goals, I could help them by empowering them on their unique path. They were still working on diet changes and increased activity, but surgery would be the catalyst that took them from struggle to success—better health, fewer pills, disease in remission, and improved quality of life. If I genuinely cared about helping people feel better, why wouldn't I want them to experience this?

This newfound understanding sparked my desire to make a difference for those who felt trapped and alone in their weight struggles. Of course, weight loss surgery was right for some, but not others. Surgeons, insurance companies, and governing bodies all have criteria that help determine if a patient is an appropriate candidate. It wasn't up to me to tell them whether or not surgery was the solution for them. That was between them, their loved ones, and their physicians. **I realized that my job was to guide and support patients on *their* terms, not mine.**

Driven by this conviction, and with the encouragement of our bariatric surgeon, I studied to become a certified bariatric nurse. I immersed myself in this specialized field, learning about the various surgical procedures, the physiological and psychological aspects of obesity, and the comprehensive care required to support our patients.

In 2013, I hung on every word when we, as a bariatric team, attended our first annual conference held by the American Society for Metabolic and Bariatric Surgery (ASMBS) and The Obesity Society (TOS) in Atlanta. I knew I was where I was supposed to be, and I was overjoyed. Counseling patients as a bariatric nurse was a role that allowed me to combine my love for nursing and my patients with my belief in the power of healthy lifestyle habits.

Now, I picture Janet healthy and glowing. Her husband admiringly tells her, "You're such a bombshell," as she heads out the door in the morning with a smile. This time, **the bombshell is the beautiful person she has become inside and out, rather than her words of surrender, as she told me she was considering weight loss surgery**. She is enjoying her life, feeling more energy and confidence, and doing the things she loves most with greater ease. This is where bariatric surgery can lead those who implement lasting change, as she did.

CHANGING THE WAY WE THINK

Still, it saddens me to acknowledge that many individuals who are considering or who have already benefited from weight loss surgery continue to face unfair judgment from those they turn to for support. It's the same type of scrutiny that I passed on to Janet decades ago, triggered by my misconceptions and misguided beliefs.

Heartbreakingly, patients regularly confide in me that they don't plan on telling anyone they are having surgery because they know there will be opposition. Such discrimination can be harmful, hindering individuals from seeking the help they need and deserve.

My experiences have taught me the importance of empathy and providing a safe space for individuals to share their struggles and aspirations. Through this book, I will challenge the stigma surrounding weight loss surgery for many and foster a more compassionate and supportive environment. I want to empower individuals to make informed decisions about their health, free from bias.

So, to anyone who has ever felt scrutinized or misunderstood, know you are not alone. We all deserve compassion and support as we work toward a better, healthier, and more fulfilling life. Let's bridge the gap between knowledge and understanding to create a process that goes beyond the surface-level advice often given in the health and wellness field.

Let's set the stage for **your positive outcome** with a **positive mindset**. We will start by addressing common myths and providing new perspectives. The information in these chapters may spark further questions. Please write them down and take them to your bariatric team if you decide to have surgery.

Chapter 2

Shake It Off: Seven Misconceptions

If you are positive, you'll see opportunities instead of obstacles.
—Widad Akreyi

Sasha entered my office and sat down with a look of paranoia as I closed the door. As a hospital employee, she knew a lot of the staff in the building and many of our patients. She leaned forward and stated, "I just want to make sure that no one knows I'm doing this." She acted ashamed, as if considering a bariatric procedure was an admission of failure and defeat. I responded, "I assure you, as we discussed on the phone, that only bariatric team members will know why you are here." I wished I could help her understand the support and encouragement she could gain by letting those who care about her know she was coming to us for help.

As a nurse, I am bound by HIPAA and strict moral and ethical codes to keep patients' privacy at the forefront of our practice. I took Sasha's concerns very seriously, but seeing her hide and feel alone during her preoperative preparation was hard. Where did this myth that weight loss surgery is something to be ashamed of come from?

As a young fitness and nutrition professional, I had minimal understanding of bariatric surgery and its benefits. I can think of various experiences that led to my misunderstanding—a neighbor who had surgery at a young age and became too thin and unhealthy looking, college courses that preached the eat less, exercise more approach, and the fact that I just had no idea how much a bariatric patient has to do in order to be successful.

Let's examine common misconceptions about weight loss surgery. Then, we will reframe them to create a success-driven mindset for your journey.

***

<u>Misconception #1: If I Need Surgery, I Must Be a Failure</u>

When we find ourselves at a dead end—up against a wall—**there is an opportunity for learning and growth**. It's time to gain new skills, learn from our mistakes, and start climbing.

As previously mentioned, modifiable and non-modifiable factors contribute to our weight and overall health. Some modifiable factors are diet, physical activity, sleep, stress, education, and living environment. Examples of non-modifiable factors include our age, genetics, race, ethnicity, and sex assigned at birth.

Medications can also play a role. Often, we have the option of choosing from different medications within a drug class, enabling us to prevent certain side effects. But sometimes, there is no alternative to life-saving drugs, and patients must suffer the side effects, such as weight gain.

For many of you, the non-modifiable factors, or the things you cannot change, impact your health more than the modifiable ones. That is not your fault. I know so many of you have dieted and exercised to the point of exhaustion and have lost the same twenty or thirty pounds over and over again. You are not alone. Do everything you can to develop healthy habits, but it is OK to need additional tools.

As the famous quote attributed to Albert Einstein says, "You never fail until you stop trying." I can't tell you how often I have used this quote with patients who, like Sasha, came to me feeling deflated and defeated. Have hope—you are not a failure!

Let's reframe our thinking by replacing this misconception with a helpful statement. Cross out Misconception #1. Yes, take a pen and cross it out. Then please replace that idea with the following statement:

> **Reframe #1:**
> **I AM BRAVE FOR SEEKING MEDICAL HELP. MY HARD WORK AND DEDICATION WILL LEAD TO MY SUCCESS!**

Misconception #2: Weight Loss Surgery Is the Easy Way Out

This is probably the most harmful and widely held misconception. But not everywhere, as I learned from a friend in Los Angeles, where bariatric surgery is a mainstream solution, and people recognize its benefits. Unfortunately, this misconception is still common in more rural areas, possibly due to less access to healthcare, fewer educational resources, or social and economic factors.

There truly is nothing easy about weight loss surgery. It is a detailed process that we will break down in Part 2. Not only that, but bariatric surgery is just one tool in the weight loss toolbelt that we strive to supply patients with as bariatric professionals. To succeed, patients start working on lifestyle changes before surgery. The preoperative process can last three to six months as you meet with your surgeon, nutritionist, mental health provider, and other care providers. Eating smaller portions and increasing activity are encouraged early on, as well as eliminating junk food and dining out less.

There are many more reasons why surgery is not the easy way out, as you will learn. The changes created by weight loss surgery are lifelong and add a new element to already challenging lives. Let this knowledge empower you to do it right. Create the habits, rally your support, and help them change with you!

Please cross out Misconception #2. Now, let's reframe it with this statement:

> **Reframe #2:**
> **THE BARIATRIC PATH IS NOT EASY, BUT I WILL LEARN AND GROW AS I OVERCOME ITS CHALLENGES, ENJOYING BETTER HEALTH AND QUALITY OF LIFE!**

Misconception #3: People Who Have Weight Loss Surgery Are Lazy and Unmotivated

This one hurts my heart. I have felt embarrassed and guilty as patients have told me with frustration how much they are working out and watching what they eat. But they still can't lose the weight—some of my patients are more active than I am! I think it's safe to say that most of us have abused food at one point or another through overeating or binging. And we all go through periods of having greater or less motivation.

Patients may have dealt with severe life stressors or trauma that we are unaware of. Many suffer from clinical eating disorders and have worked hard to overcome them. Add the genetic likelihood for weight gain, and without proper support, they are fighting an uphill battle. What if every time we experienced a major life trial, we gained a green spot on our face? Would we point a finger and judge people based on their spots? NO. We would show empathy and encouragement because we all have green spots! We all wear our struggles and traumas differently. Unfortunately, some are more visible than others.

I remember reading an article where Gwyneth Paltrow talked about filming the movie *Shallow Hal*. She wore a suit and prosthetics to make her look obese in parts of the movie. In the article, Gwyneth spoke about wearing the suit off-camera and how people treated her, not recognizing who she was. "It was so sad. It was so disturbing. No one would make eye contact with me because I was obese. I felt humiliated."[3] It was a very eye-opening experience for her.

Similarly, one of my patients said people had difficulty making eye contact with her before surgery, even during a conversation! She often felt ignored or avoided and also said that when she shopped for clothes, no one wanted to help her. Now, she reports that since losing her excess weight, people smile at her a lot more and make eye contact without hesitation. I will never understand how one can justify treating another poorly or differently based on appearance, but that is another book.

And by the way, when I say obese, I'm not just talking about severe obesity. You may be one of the many shocked to discover that your body mass index (BMI) weight classification qualifies you for surgical intervention. I will explain the BMI more in the next section.

The idea that our weight is a *direct* reflection of our motivation, activity level, or worthiness of respect is absurd. **Obesity does not equal laziness**. Eating less and exercising more does not work for everyone! There is so much more going on than calories in and calories out.

Please cross out Misconception #3 and reframe it with this statement:

> **Reframe #3:**
> **SUCCESSFUL WEIGHT LOSS SURGERY PATIENTS ARE HIGHLY MOTIVATED, HAVING COMMITTED TO A LIFE OF BETTER FOOD CHOICES AND REGULAR ACTIVITY!**

Misconception #4: Weight Loss Surgery Guarantees Permanent Weight Loss

While you can rest assured with almost absolute certainty that you will lose weight after a surgical weight loss procedure, the only guarantee you will keep the weight off is to develop healthy eating and activity routines. Likewise, **following up with your surgeon, primary care provider, and specialists is critical** to achieving your goals.

The weight loss surgery will not do all the work. Still, your rapid weight loss in the months after surgery will finally give you the momentum you need, making it easier to solidify healthy **bariatric habits as a permanent part of your lifestyle**. Start working on your behaviors now. The more practice you have before surgery, the easier it will be afterward.

Please cross out the misconception and reframe the idea:

> **Reframe #4:**
> **WEIGHT LOSS SURGERY IS A TOOL THAT CAN HELP ME ACHIEVE MY GOALS AS I STRIVE TO BUILD LIFELONG HEALTHY HABITS!**

Misconception #5: Bariatric Patients Suffer from Starvation and Poor Nutrition

You may have had the experience, as I did, of observing someone lose weight rapidly after weight loss surgery and become unhealthy-looking. It takes a lot of effort to follow your diet stages properly after surgery and keep up with hydration and nutrition.

I cannot stress enough the importance of planning ahead and understanding the instructions you receive. Your surgeon and your bariatric team want you to succeed! Closely following instructions can make the difference between a smooth recovery and a bumpy postoperative road. And who wants to ride on a bumpy road after having stomach surgery? Sorry, bad joke—but true!

Bariatric supplements are formulated specifically for different procedures. Extensive research has been performed to identify and prevent nutrient deficiencies after weight loss surgery. We know which vitamins and minerals are absorbed in specific areas of the digestive tract, so bariatric vitamin regimens are created based on your health history and which procedure you have. This is determined by how the stomach and sometimes the small intestine are modified during surgery. We have evidence-based guidelines to help minimize your risk for nutrition problems and unhealthy weight loss.

Of course, there can be complications. But major complications are rare at only four percent, according to the most recent numbers from the ASMBS.[4] If you and your physicians have determined that the benefits outweigh the risks (there are always risks in any surgery), you are a good candidate for surgery, AND you are willing to adhere to your care regimen, there is no reason you shouldn't expect to lose weight and be healthier.

It can be helpful to start trying bariatric vitamins now. You can find them in liquid, tablet, capsule, and chewable forms. Some of the soft chews are delicious, almost like a Mamba candy (a creamier, softer version of a Starburst) if you loved those as a kid like I did. Your dietician or surgeon can often provide samples, or you can reach out to individual vitamin companies for coupons or samples.

Popular brands are Bariatric Advantage, Celebrate, Bariatric Fusion, Barimelts, Bariatric Pal, and Unjury. Many of them offer additional products besides vitamins. I have tried samples of all these brands, and most taste good! However, it all comes down to your personal taste.

Your protein intake and levels are used to monitor for malnutrition after surgery, in addition to your micronutrient (vitamin and mineral) intake and levels. Your bariatric team will advise you on what to look for in supplemental protein shakes. You may want to start trying some now. But don't go and buy cases of your favorite shake; your taste may change after surgery. Again, coupons may be available from your dietician or surgeon. You can also find them online or contact manufacturers directly for coupons and discount codes.

Your bariatric surgeon will recommend when and how long you need vitamin, mineral, and protein supplements. Some will be lifelong, others may not. They will also order blood work routinely after surgery to ensure you are healthy. But, if at any point you feel like you are suffering from poor nutrition, you should reach out to a member of your bariatric team. You are your best advocate—only you know how you feel.

Please cross out Misconception #5 and reframe it:

> **Reframe #5:**
> **I CAN STAY HEALTHY AND MINIMIZE PROBLEMS AFTER BARIATRIC SURGERY BY FOLLOWING MY CARE INSTRUCTIONS AND MEETING WITH MY HEALTHCARE PROVIDERS!**

Misconception #6: I Won't Be Able to Eat the Foods I Love or Enjoy Food Anymore

Some patients recommend having a "food funeral" ceremony prior to bariatric surgery. While your relationship with food will change, and you should say goodbye to certain unhealthy foods, there is no need to mourn! People who have weight loss surgery can eat the same foods as everyone else, just in smaller portions.

Of course, some foods are discouraged, such as high-fat, high-sugar, fast food, and empty-calorie or junk foods. But those are things you will have eliminated from your diet before surgery with the help of your bariatric team.

If you feel hooked on some of these foods, you can use a meal plan to help implement healthy eating habits. Meal plans are helpful because you don't have to think about what you eat. Just plan ahead and stick with it. It can be easier to say no when something is not on your plan. Seek guidance from your dietician for meal planning. You can also find sample meal plans online, but please don't follow bariatric meal plans before surgery. They do not contain enough calories and will negatively affect your metabolism.

Focus on what you add, not what you are taking away. By eliminating unhealthy foods and adding healthier options before surgery, you will set yourself up for success, experience fewer cravings, and soon feel more satisfied and nourished!

As far as enjoying food goes, if you follow your bariatric guidelines, you can enjoy food AND the benefit of filling up faster. It will feel like you are not eating very much—you're not! But trust the research and physiological effects of the surgery. Focus on protein, nutrition, and hydration, and savor every bite. You will develop a new and better relationship with food as you adhere to bariatric guidelines.

I will mention that there are instances where patients no longer tolerate certain foods after surgery. But in my experience, this is the exception, not the norm. Food intolerance is often related to underlying problems like lactose intolerance, eating gas-forming foods, eating too fast, or not chewing well. There are ways we can address and alleviate these types of intolerances.

Additionally, foods high in carbohydrates, such as sugar, potatoes, and white flour, can cause dumping syndrome (dizziness, nausea, diarrhea, and more) after bariatric surgery.[5] Your surgeon will talk to you more about dumping syndrome if this is a consideration with your chosen procedure. However, it can be an advantage, and some patients choose procedures likely to cause dumping syndrome to help them avoid sweets and other unhealthy carbohydrates.

Please cross out the misconception and replace it with this:

> **Reframe #6:**
> **AS I EAT SLOWLY, CHEW WELL, AND CHOOSE APPROPRIATE FOODS, I WILL ENJOY MEALS AND CREATE A NEW, HEALTHY RELATIONSHIP WITH FOOD!** (YES, YOU CAN EAT STEAK—just not right away)

Misconception #7: People Who Have Bariatric Surgery Do It for Their Appearance

In my ten years of sitting down with pre-surgery patients and asking them why they are considering weight loss surgery, TWO have mentioned anything about their appearance. They just want to be healthy!

They are tired of feeling stuck. They are tired of feeling exhausted and unwell. They want to enjoy the things they love again, move with ease, bend over and tie their shoes, or sit in a restaurant booth. Patients want to care for themselves and their loved ones. They want to be around to see their children get married and have children of their own. They want to get down on the floor (and more importantly, be able to get back up) and play with their grandchildren.

Weight loss surgery can help propel you toward improved quality of life. You are not superficial or cheating if you have weight loss surgery. You are taking on the vast responsibility of caring for your body and your future well-being.

Please cross out Misconception #7 and reframe:

> **Reframe #7:**
> **BARIATRIC SURGERY IS ABOUT BETTER HEALTH AND QUALITY OF LIFE, AND IF I LOOK GREAT IN THE PROCESS, THAT'S A BONUS!**

Now that we've reframed some of the most common misconceptions about weight loss surgery, let's turn to advice from bariatric care team members. Following are the most important things they want you to know before deciding to have weight loss surgery.

Chapter 3

Advice from Bariatric Care Providers

An investment in knowledge pays the best interest.
— Benjamin Franklin

I asked surgeons and bariatric team members for their advice to patients before having surgery. Their answers may surprise you and will help give you a head start. I also include a few things I have seen surgeons become the most frustrated by. Of course, they can't express that frustration to the patient, so the nurse quickly learns how to help prevent these situations. Not that surgeons get mad at their patients, but like anyone, they will have frustrations now and then.

DO YOUR RESEARCH AND FIND OUT WHAT'S BEST FOR YOU

When researching weight loss surgery, read from reputable websites. I will list several in the resources section. Reading from websites that end in .org, .gov, or .edu will provide you with the most reliable information. Remember that websites ending in .com are "commercial"; they are for-profit companies. So, while they may have exciting and nice-looking content, they're not the most reliable regarding the facts.

Blogs are also a popular resource for interesting information. But as I have implied, you need to read between the lines. Some content can serve the person who wrote it as advertising, venting, or boasting, so you'll likely not get the whole story. You may learn more about what *not* to do on blogs, as patients often share their blunders. That is not to say that it isn't helpful, but for accuracy, stick with the information provided by your bariatric surgeon and other reputable sources.

While researching, you will read about several bariatric surgical procedures. It is essential to choose the procedure that is best for you. Some are more invasive—some are less invasive. They all have their pros and cons as well as risks and benefits. While your surgeon will discuss the details of the procedures with you, most patients have one or two in mind before they meet with their surgeon for the first time.

The two most commonly performed procedures are the laparoscopic vertical sleeve gastrectomy (LVSG) and the laparoscopic Roux en Y gastric bypass (LRYGB). I will refer to them as the sleeve and the bypass. Laparoscopic means the procedure is minimally invasive, using small incisions and access ports rather than a large, open abdominal incision. It is important to note, however, that laparoscopic procedures can always turn into "open" procedures if the surgeon deems it necessary, such as in the case of an emergency. Most bariatric surgeries are laparoscopic.

Robotic-assisted laparoscopic surgeries are now commonly performed as well. Both are minimally invasive. I have enjoyed observing both types of surgery in the operating room. I assure you the surgeon is in complete control the entire time. The robotic arms do not operate independently. They are controlled directly by the surgeon and provide an increased range of motion. Look it up on YouTube—it's really cool! Again, choose a video from a reputable source, such as a hospital or a health organization.

Another critical aspect is to consider your health history as you research. For example, if you suffer from gastroesophageal reflux disease (GERD), having the gastric bypass can help alleviate symptoms, whereas having the sleeve is more likely to increase GERD symptoms.[6] Some patients with GERD or acid reflux opt to have the sleeve anyway because it is less invasive. Doing so will require your diligence in reporting and treating increased symptoms to prevent dangerous ulcers.

Furthermore, you may read about biliopancreatic diversion (BPD) or biliopancreatic diversion with duodenal switch (BPD-DS). These two procedures are *highly* malabsorptive (meaning they limit nutrient absorption). They can be associated with greater weight loss, but as such, they also contain a greater risk for nutritional deficiencies and other complications such as diarrhea.[7] Consequently, I do not include them as part of our discussion.

Another procedure, gastric banding, which is purely restrictive (only limits the *amount* you can eat), has its own disadvantages. Gastric bands can migrate over time, leading to pain, nausea, digestive problems, and gastric or stomach erosion. I have witnessed the agony that patients suffer from band migration or slippage AND the relief they experience after its removal. When an improperly positioned gastric band is removed, these patients feel normal again—sometimes after years of suffering.

Most surgeons are no longer performing gastric banding. They are only removing the bands. Furthermore, gastric banding will not lead to direct improvements in disease processes like diabetes and hypertension (high blood pressure). Whereas **restrictive *and* malabsorptive** bariatric procedures like the sleeve, bypass, and BPDs lead to almost immediate **diabetes in remission and improvements in hypertension** in most cases.[8] Discuss considerations like these with your doctors and surgeon because the more you understand beforehand, the better.

The amount of weight loss you can expect is another essential part of your research. Some procedures will likely cause more weight loss early on, which can have benefits and risks. Other procedures are equally effective long term but less aggressive early on. Likewise, you can discuss these factors with your surgeon to determine what's right for you.

I hope by now you can see the benefits of thorough research. Come to your surgeon with a good knowledge foundation and questions to ask. You will have a productive consultation.

NOT EVERYONE SUFFERING FROM OBESITY SHOULD HAVE SURGERY

Lance had struggled with his weight since he was a child. Obesity ran in his family, and they all suffered its effects. He was disabled and on Medicare. He admitted that it was long past time to do something about his weight, but he struggled to make changes. There were days when he slept all day, woke up, ate a large meal of fast food and soda, then went back to bed. He had diabetes and ran the risk of having severe heart failure. His wife worked hard to provide healthy options, but sadly, Lance was full of excuses.

He blamed his weight and his health on everyone and everything but himself. Some of it *was* beyond his control. But he was unwilling to do his part to make better choices and get out of bed every day (which he could physically do). As Lance continued to gain weight, he became dependent on oxygen and more medications, which led to more side effects such as fatigue—it was a downward spiral.

We met with and coached Lance for years before we finally had to turn him away due to multiple no-show appointments. He always called days later to reschedule, and the excuses never stopped. I hope Lance can one day find the willpower to change, but his lack of responsibility and desire to do his part meant he would likely end up back where he started. In his circumstances, weight loss surgery was not an option.

This is a tough example, but it demonstrates the importance of having the right attitude for surgery. Your surgeon does not want to perform a major procedure on someone unlikely to succeed. As much as we care for and believe in our patients, there is a responsibility to weigh the risks versus the benefits to ensure surgery is safe. As a bariatric team, nurses, dieticians, mental health professionals, and other care providers communicate with your surgeon to aid them in their decision-making.

Next, let's discuss the physical reasons why surgery might not be appropriate. According to a recent study, medical conditions that might prevent you from being a candidate for surgery include severe heart failure, unstable coronary artery disease, end-stage lung disease, active cancer treatment, portal hypertension, drug/alcohol dependency, and impaired intellectual capacity. The bypass procedure is also not recommended for patients with Crohn's disease.[9]

Maintaining an open discussion with your primary care provider regarding your considerations for weight loss surgery is essential. Suppose weight loss surgery is not an option due to your current health. In that case, they can steer you in another direction that will be beneficial. Although, in my experience, patients are most commonly denied bariatric surgery due to unmet insurance requirements. I will discuss how to navigate that obstacle in Chapters 4 and 5.

If you find out you are not a candidate for weight loss surgery, please don't let this discourage you. I challenge you to start your own bariatric journey without surgery. **Gain the tools that can help surgical and non-surgical patients alike.** Some potential patients no longer need or want surgery after they start making lifestyle changes and experience some weight loss. Keep open-minded, but also look at the long-term picture and really figure out what is best for you in your current circumstances.

YOU NEED TO BE IN THE RIGHT PLACE MENTALLY

This topic ties right in with the previous one. You need to be sure that surgery is the right choice, both physically *and* mentally. If you aren't ready for change, it's probably not the right time for weight loss surgery.

I have met with many individuals who are the perfect candidates for bariatric surgery on paper. Yet, they are currently experiencing too many life stressors to be able to commit to having a successful surgery outcome. Most of them know deep down that their heart is not in it, but they are desperate for help. I'm not saying you can't get there if you are in this situation, but it will take time and effort. You need to be open and honest with your doctors, mental health providers, dieticians, and nurses so that they can help you. Remember, we want you to succeed as much as you do, but steps or resources may get left out if we don't have the whole picture.

To get in the right place mentally, turn to loved ones whose insights and opinions you can trust and make yourself accountable. The more valuable team members you have, the more they can guide and elevate you toward your goals.

Every patient is different, but what you have in common is what matters—your determination and commitment. Preoperative preparation time frames vary significantly from person to person. If you take longer to get in the right place mentally and deal with life stressors before surgery, there is nothing wrong with you. In my experience, you are **more likely to succeed** because of your extra effort. And you will look back with gratitude for the time you had to prepare for the rest of your amazing life.

IT'S NOT A GIVEN THAT YOU WILL SUCCEED—IT TAKES WORK

Tools are not made to sit in a tool belt. They are meant to be pulled out and used—the right tool for the right job. Imagine a construction worker showing up at the site and pulling out a saw to hammer the nails in place. I don't see that project getting completed anytime soon, do you?

What are you trying to build? What is the outcome that you desire? Get specific, gain the tools, make a plan, and get to work. We can give you the tools and teach you how to use them, but you must do the work to create your marvelous outcome. You must practice, repeat, and refine those skills to construct your improved health and well-being.

As with any new project, there will be unforeseen trials. The best you can do is lay the framework and keep at it. When challenges arise, turn to your healthcare team and your personal support system to guide you. By choosing the bariatric path, you join millions of patients and healthcare providers who offer experience, support, and encouragement.

SURGERY IS PERMANENT

Okay, most surgery is permanent. Some procedures, such as the gastric balloon or gastric band, are meant to be temporary or can be reversed. There is also a conversion from gastric sleeve to bypass; however, it is highly *inadvisable* to pursue a bariatric procedure while thinking in the back of your mind that if it doesn't work out, you can have another surgery to fix it.

Some surgeries and surgical aspects truly are permanent. For example, a sleeve gastrectomy creates a staple line along the lower border of the stomach, allowing for the removal of approximately seventy-five percent of the stomach. That portion of your stomach is removed from your body. You cannot get it back.

While you may spend months or years preparing for surgery and feel ready to have had it yesterday, please bear in mind that there is no way to be prepared for every little detail you encounter throughout the process. Most patients have an, "Oh, no! What have I done?" moment shortly after surgery. It is typically overcome as they recover and start to observe weight loss. Still, talk to someone about how you are feeling—your nurse, surgeon, and online and hospital support groups are invaluable. You don't need to feel alone.

There will always be uncertainty going into something as serious as weight loss surgery. One of my patients called it "nervouscited" (nervous but excited), which I believe sums it up perfectly. I hope you will put plenty of thought into preparation if you decide to have weight loss surgery. I also hope you will be excited to enjoy the benefits.

SWITCH GEARS IF NECESSARY AND GIVE IT YOUR ALL

This section is for patients who may have found themselves pursuing surgery out of necessity rather than the desire to have weight loss surgery. Some patients come to us more at the recommendation of another physician than their personal preference.

Many of you suffer from impaired mobility and pain due to joint problems. Often, orthopedic surgeons refer patients to bariatric surgeons because they are required to lose weight before joint replacement or spinal procedures (less weight is less stress on the bones). Many patients come to us with specific BMIs (usually around 50) that their surgeon requires them to achieve before they can have their orthopedic surgery.

Switching gears and focusing on a successful bariatric course can be difficult if you are one of these patients. It's hard not to have tunnel vision when you are suffering from pain or illness, but try to have a far-reaching perspective. By preparing for weight loss surgery, you are working toward improvements not only in your pain and quality of life but also in your overall health. The effects of bariatric surgery may additionally prevent future disease processes for you.

More doors are opening, so I encourage you to maximize this opportunity.

Giving it your all is about fully committing yourself to a goal or endeavor. It means giving your absolute best, stepping outside your comfort zone, and pushing through any barriers. So go all in, give it your all, and watch as your determination and commitment lead you to a better life.

READ AND REREAD YOUR PATIENT GUIDES AND INSTRUCTIONS

You should receive a manual or guide when you start your bariatric program. Please read it to understand surgical stages and their instructions before having surgery. Bring any questions to your bariatric team. Doing so can save time and frustration after surgery. A nurse or dietician can usually answer your questions, or they'll provide you with an answer from the surgeon.

Surgeons are sometimes unavailable for extended periods because they are in the operating room, so please clarify as much information as possible *before* surgery. Of course, if there is an emergency, there is always a surgeon covering or on call. You should always call your surgeon's office first. If it hasn't been long since your hospital discharge, and it's the weekend (the office is closed), you can call the after-hours line or the nurses' station at the hospital.

What's more, have your loved one or support person (whoever will be helping you most after surgery) read your instructions. It is hard to keep track of things when you are tired, sore, and often a little loopy after anesthesia and pain medication. So, **having another set of ears and eyes is vital**. They will have questions of their own, so be ready to bring those to the appointments with your surgeon. Some surgeons will even require you to have a support person with you each time you meet with them.

You will receive different sets of instructions at various stages, so try to familiarize yourself with each before your next appointment. It will make things easier and more understandable as you build on your progress. Also, please don't replace information you receive from your surgeon with something you read online—for example—the steps of your preoperative diet. Your surgeon will give you personalized instructions based on *your* needs; please trust them.

MEET WITH YOUR PRIMARY CARE PROVIDER & SPECIALISTS BEFORE SURGERY

Your care providers need to be aware that you are pursuing weight loss surgery. They may need to make medication adjustments and plan your continued care around surgery. They may also recommend specific tests or imaging before surgery. Suppose you suffer from lung disease, such as COPD, and you see a pulmonologist. Your pulmonologist may order a pulmonary function test to ensure you will tolerate anesthesia during surgery.

Your surgeon may also request tests to be completed by these specialists. For example, if you see a cardiologist regularly for a heart condition, you may need a stress test or echocardiogram before surgery. Your specialist can order these tests at your next routine visit, or you can call to schedule an appointment. You will also want to have your annual blood work with your primary care provider early on so you have a baseline for values like your hemoglobin A1c (a diabetes marker) and your cholesterol levels.

If you aren't sure if your surgeon requires you to see specialists, be sure to ask at your initial consultation. I have seen patients have to leave the surgeon's office and reschedule for weeks later because they forgot to follow up with another doctor. Trust me, surgeons hate having to do this, as it's a waste of time for you and for them. It makes sense, right? Remember, this is the rest of your life, and **you want to be sure that you are in optimal health and condition for surgery**.

HONESTY IS KEY

Last but not least, please be honest. If we don't know you are struggling with something, we can't help you. We are not here to judge you but to support you in achieving your goals. Trust me, anything that you struggle with that is not addressed before surgery won't automatically disappear after surgery. Whether it's eating too fast, overindulging in sweets, emotional eating, or understanding nutrition labels—it will still be a struggle. We have so many resources. Please allow us the opportunity to assist you.

Part 2: DIRECTION

In 2022, there were major changes to bariatric guidelines that made it possible for millions of patients to qualify for surgery who had previously been turned away. As new research emerges, the bariatric process is constantly changing. If you decide that surgery is right and you encounter obstacles on your way, be patient. Keep researching and trying new approaches.

Also, please be advised that this guidance is intended only for adults. Adolescents may qualify for weight loss surgery under strict guidelines, but maturing bodies and minds are so vulnerable. Surgery should only be considered after all efforts have been made for healthy lifestyle education and practice, as well as behavioral counseling. One study concluded that it is critical for adolescent patients undergoing bariatric surgery to be evaluated and monitored by clinicians for suicidal ideation and behaviors.[10]

Please do not act too soon if you are concerned about your teenager suffering from obesity. Surgery will affect them for the rest of their life. In my humble opinion, it is a choice that should be made as an emotionally mature adult only, unless there are special health considerations. In that case, please involve as many experts as possible to ensure it is the right decision.

As a parent and a professional who has studied disordered eating, I must caution that even suggesting an adolescent should consider bariatric surgery can severely damage their already fragile self-esteem. You can model good habits. Explore every avenue, but if surgery is deemed necessary, be sure to find a surgical team with substantial experience treating adolescents suffering from obesity.

Now, this section contains a lot of details. I have included my every consideration as a bariatric nurse, clinical coordinator, and health coach to assist you in pursuing surgery if it's right for you. I don't claim to be the foremost expert. However, I do have a unique perspective, having counseled patients one-on-one from start to finish under the direction of bariatric surgeons. I have walked with them, overcoming the obstacles.

Remember to not get ahead of yourself—focus on one step at a time, and utilize your bariatric team when you get overwhelmed. The time and energy you spend preparing for surgery are a worthy investment in your future.

Chapter 4

Timing Is Everything: How to Qualify

The two most powerful warriors are patience and time.
— Leo Tolstoy

Emilia worked in a convenience store and knew she drank too much soda. Losing weight had become important to her, so she was ready to change. She battled her insurance company for almost two years because her BMI was borderline for weight loss surgery qualification.

During the first several months of her journey, as she worked on cutting out soda and adding more protein to her diet preoperatively, she lost a few pounds. That weight loss dropped her BMI out of the qualifying range, and heartbroken, she left the bariatric program. It's not that Emilia wasn't happy with her weight loss. She felt better, but she knew the weight would come back as it always did.

She suffered from a hereditary type of obesity called central obesity. Often, these patients have thinner legs and arms, but their midsection is noticeably round.

The type of fat that contributes to much of the size of the round belly is called visceral fat. It is the type that surrounds and protects your organs behind the abdominal wall rather than the subcutaneous fat that lies directly under your skin. Visceral fat in excess is the most dangerous type of body fat, as it is linked to serious health conditions like type 2 diabetes, heart disease, and stroke.[11]

Emilia was tired of people telling her she looked fine and didn't need weight loss surgery when she knew the dangers of her condition. She had lost her dad prematurely to a heart attack, and fear of suffering the same fate had almost overtaken her at this point. She was forty-four. Her dad died at age forty-six.

Just as she knew it would, the weight slowly returned, even as she practiced her new eating habits and stayed active. She called us for another consultation and learned that her BMI once again qualified her for bariatric surgery. Emilia had her surgery just before her forty-sixth birthday, and years later, she continues to enjoy improved health and energy, newfound confidence, and a significantly reduced risk for heart disease.

BMI AND HEALTH CONDITIONS

In the medical field, we use body mass index (BMI) tables to classify your weight. The BMI is a height-to-weight ratio (your weight in kilograms divided by your height in meters squared). This classification system is not flawless, as it does not consider body composition. So, for example, someone who is not very tall and has significant muscle mass may be classified as obese. Conversely, someone who is very tall and has little muscle mass and excess fat could be classified as healthy. It's imperfect, but it's what we have.

Methods for body composition analysis can provide reliable information about your health concerning lean versus fat mass. However, accurate body composition analysis can be expensive, and the less expensive options, such as body fat percent testing, can be inaccurate. For these reasons, we primarily use the BMI.

You can look up "BMI calculator" on the internet for easy results using your height in inches and weight in pounds or using the metric system. A BMI over 30 is considered obese, but remember, this is just a height-to-weight ratio. Your overall health is what's most important. Ultimately, your insurance company and your surgeon will determine if you qualify for surgery. Your insurance will have its criteria regarding who qualifies for surgery and under which circumstances they will offer coverage benefits.

Until recently, you needed a BMI of 35-39.9 and at least one obesity-related condition or **comorbidity** OR a BMI over 40 with or without comorbidities to qualify for bariatric surgery. Examples of comorbidities are type 2 diabetes, high blood pressure, heart disease, and obstructive sleep apnea. However, new

TIMING IS EVERYTHING: HOW TO QUALIFY

research has led to changes in the guidelines by the American Society for Metabolic and Bariatric Surgery (ASMBS).[12]

This is great news for the many patients I have observed battling BMIs in the low 30s. Time and time again, I have met with patients who have struggled with their weight for years or even decades. They may have been told they are pre-diabetic or showing signs of obstructive sleep apnea but don't yet have an official diagnosis. They are scared and want to do something about their weight to prevent compounding health problems, but they don't qualify for bariatric surgery.

Similarly, new patients come in with a BMI of just over 35 or 36, then lose weight during preparation for surgery and no longer qualify, like Emilia. Seeing these patients who were ready for help and change have to be turned away has been troubling. If you are told that your BMI has to be 35 or above, keep looking for a surgeon or insurance coverage that utilizes these new guidelines.

Please note that insurance companies can take months or years to update their coverage policies based on new guidelines and research. Still, some have already included bariatric coverage for individuals with a **BMI of 30 if they have type 2 diabetes or are unable to achieve "substantial or durable weight loss or comorbidity improvement using non-surgical methods,"** referring back to the ASMBS guidelines.

The ASMBS also recommends metabolic and bariatric surgery (MBS) or weight loss surgery for adults with a BMI of 35 or greater, whether or not they have obesity-related conditions. If your BMI is over 40, you typically should not have trouble qualifying for surgery if it is included in your insurance benefits.

PREVIOUS WEIGHT LOSS ATTEMPTS

Your surgeon and your insurance company will want to know what you have tried in the past to lose weight. Ensure that you can recall which diets you have used, as well as any exercise programs, personal trainers, and medically supervised weight loss programs. If you have official documentation from a weight loss program, bring it with you. Even better, if you have discussed your weight struggles with your primary care provider and they have kept a record, it can be submitted to your insurance. Be sure to **include your starting weight, how much weight you lost, and how long you kept it off.**

Some insurances require your history of obesity to be documented for as long as five years. If you can provide this for your bariatric team, it can help determine that your surgery is medically necessary. If you don't have a five-year history, don't stress; bring what you have, and your surgeon will ask you for more details to help determine if surgery is right for you.

NO INSURANCE COVERAGE AND GOING TO MEXICO!

Patients who do not have insurance coverage for bariatric surgery and are paying out of pocket must still meet qualifying guidelines. Your surgeon may use the ASMBS guidelines in addition to the National Institutes of Health (NIH) guidelines or others. Your previous weight loss attempts and weight history will be considered, along with your health history, so be sure to bring this documentation to your initial consultation with your surgeon.

Certainly, many of you reading this have already considered going to Mexico or somewhere else out of the country for weight loss surgery. This is a popular solution for patients who discover they do not have insurance coverage for bariatric procedures.

Many patients who travel for surgery do well and report having a great experience. But here's the thing—I can't help but wonder if they know what they are missing out on, not having a complete, team approach involving their local healthcare providers. I recall one woman who started coming to our local support groups shortly after her surgery in Mexico. She worked hard to succeed, continually making positive changes, and has achieved sustained weight loss.

Alternatively, many patients have had negative experiences and bad surgical outcomes. Of course, we know this can happen anywhere, so **do your homework, regardless of whether you are staying local or traveling abroad for surgery.** Whatever you decide, find a reputable surgeon, program, and facility. Read reviews, check success rates, verify credentials, and ask questions in online forums like Facebook groups or Instagram pages.

One of the advantages of having weight loss surgery in Mexico is that it is cheaper if you have to pay out of pocket, meaning you don't have insurance coverage. You should also consider these possible disadvantages:

    1. You will be far away from the support of family and friends if there are

problems.

2. There may be unexpected costs (hiatal hernia repairs at the time of surgery are common).

3. Regulations and standards may not be as strict.

4. The screening process to ensure your positive surgical outcome may not be sufficient.

5. There could be communication barriers.

6. Your aftercare and follow-up will be limited.

7. Your insurance will not cover any problems that could be related to your weight loss surgery afterward.

I'm not saying all of these are a given, but thorough research is required to ensure your safety.

AGE, OVERALL HEALTH, AND COMMITMENT

These are considerations that your bariatric team will weigh as they discuss the possibility of surgery with you. There is no defined upper age limit. Most insurance companies that offer bariatric benefits cover surgery for adults eighteen and older.

I have seen seventy-four-year-olds who are otherwise healthy benefit from surgical weight loss. I have also seen people as young as thirty-four who are in poor health and demonstrate low commitment to following their doctors' recommendations be turned away from bariatric surgery as an option.

Some bariatric programs may have implemented age limits, but your surgeon will carefully consider all factors affecting your outcome.

While you cannot change your age and have little ability to quickly modify your current health, coming to your initial surgical consultation prepared to discuss the lifestyle changes you are committed to making will be beneficial. **Better food choices, increased activity** (always talk to your doctor before starting an exercise routine), **quitting smoking, and reducing alcohol intake** will all help. Get specific and show your surgeon that you mean to succeed!

PSYCHOLOGICAL EVALUATION

The ASMBS recommends presurgical psychological evaluation before weight loss surgery to "provide screening and identification of risk factors or potential postoperative challenges that may contribute to a poor postoperative outcome. These factors may lead to the recommendation of additional management or intervention before and or after surgery, or, in some cases, may contraindicate surgery. The ultimate aim of these evaluations is to enhance surgical outcomes."[13]

Please don't stress if you have a history of anxiety or depression. Those will not automatically disqualify you. As outlined, any identified risk factors may simply lead to treatment recommendations before surgery. Depression and anxiety should be stable and well-managed before surgery.

Some patients see improvements in their mental health after surgery. Conversely, some patients experience increased symptoms as they navigate their bariatric lifestyle. That is why it's so important to do an honest self-assessment and **gain proper support** before surgery. I recommend speaking openly with your surgeon and psychological evaluator about your history to ensure you **have a plan for the ups and downs after surgery**.

I have only witnessed one patient told that their psychological history would prevent them from having a bariatric procedure. This young man suffered from schizophrenia, which was poorly managed. I sat in the exam room with our psychological care provider, Britney, to help her provide the physiological explanation, as outlined to me by our surgeon, for why surgery would not be safe in his condition.

It quickly became clear that the right decision had been made. The patient became argumentative, then verbally hostile, and angrily left the office, threatening to harm himself. I called the patient's emergency contact and referring physician to ensure he would be safe. It was a sad and difficult situation.

Many **patients are surprised at the support and encouragement they gain** from the psychological evaluation appointment. Many continue with the provider for ongoing counseling and enjoy significant benefits. Try not to overthink your answers on the tests they give you or to the questions they ask you in the interview process. Just answer honestly, as strange as some of the questions may be.

I don't recommend completing this evaluation before meeting with your bariatric team. Your specific program may have a list of providers with specialized training in these types of assessments. If your insurance won't cover the evaluation, online bariatric psychological care providers can perform the evaluation virtually for direct payment. If you use this route, be sure that your surgeon AND your insurance will accept this type of evaluation. Many insurance policies require specific criteria for this step in their process.

DIAGNOSTIC TESTING

If you are having trouble qualifying for weight loss surgery but know you need the additional tool, I have one last consideration: See your primary care provider to determine if you need any tests that may provide supporting evidence of your medical necessity for surgery.

You may be suffering from an obesity-related condition, or comorbidity, and don't even know it. For example, if you snore, wake up gasping, or suffer from daytime sleepiness, you may have sleep apnea and should pursue a sleep study. Or, when was the last time your blood work included a hemoglobin A1c test for diabetes? These **diagnostic tests can make the difference between a "yes" or "no" when qualifying for bariatric surgery**.

Once you've maneuvered through the qualifications, it's time to look more at how to handle insurance coverage considerations. I know it sounds crazy, but for many, dealing with insurance requirements is one of the hardest parts of preparing for weight loss surgery.

Chapter 5

Insurance Pebbles: Roll with It

Patience is bitter, but its fruit is sweet.
— Aristotle

Have you ever had a rock in your shoe? I am a big fan of Chaco sandals. They are the closest thing to not wearing shoes I have found, and I can wear them almost anywhere. Despite their versatility, I often end up with little pebbles stuck between the sole of my sandal and the bottom of my foot. Strangely, after wearing these sandals for more than twenty-five years, I hardly notice that I am walking around with a rock in my shoe. It is a minor annoyance.

Every now and then, I get fed up with the pebble and pluck it out. But because my Chaco sandals are amazing in most ways, I tolerate the occasional pebble. I have learned to work with it. Insurance is like this pebble—most of us have to learn to work with it. Troublesome as it can be, it is a valuable and necessary aspect of our healthcare.

STARTING OFF ON THE RIGHT FOOT

As clinicians, we struggle every day to ensure that medications, tests, and procedures are covered and authorized by your insurance. However, this is also *your* responsibility. I cannot stress enough the importance of becoming familiar with your policy, learning how to check for coverage, and understanding how copays, deductibles, and out-of-pocket work.

There are no guarantees that insurance will pay for everything your doctor orders, and physicians order based on medical need, not based on insurance coverage. They can change orders on items like medications if it is determined that something is not covered, but you must **be your own advocate.**

Typically, hospitals and facilities have staff that authorize diagnostic imaging and surgical procedures with your insurance. Doctor's offices generally do not have designated staff to check whether your insurance covers medications and labs *before* orders are sent. Many nurses and aides learn over time that certain insurances don't cover particular medications or labs. Still, you may not discover that something isn't covered until you end up with a bill, or sometimes, your pharmacy or lab will notify you. Ultimately, it is up to you to ask about coverage when meds, labs, tests, or procedures are ordered—or call your insurance company to ensure coverage.

With bariatric procedures, most insurance companies require **prior authorization.** That means there are criteria that you, as the patient, *and* the ordering physician must meet before your insurance will authorize coverage. The authorization request is sent after your bariatric surgeon has met with you for the final time before surgery and has ordered the procedure the two of you agreed upon. Prior authorization can take two to four weeks, and again, even though your bariatric team will compile and submit the authorization, you, as the insurance client, are responsible for ensuring that the criteria have been met.

Start now by calling your insurance company and asking them if you have coverage for weight loss surgery or check online. They may require a CPT code. I will include a few of those in the resources section and some tips on what to say when you call your insurance company. If you find out you have coverage, ask them to send you the details and requirements in writing via email or snail mail. Likewise, you can **find policy details online** using your insurance website or app.

Your bariatric team needs this information specific to your policy to help you meet the criteria and qualify for surgery. We can call or look up bariatric coverage information for most insurance companies. But you have access to *your specific policy*, so please obtain the information, read it, and bring it to your surgeon's office.

INSURANCE PEBBLES: ROLL WITH IT

KEEP CLIMBING

Reviewing your insurance criteria periodically throughout your preoperative preparation can be helpful. Things change—especially at the beginning of a new year after updates have been applied. As you may know, insurance policy wording is NOT easy to read and understand, so get help from the insurance coordinator on your bariatric team and work with your care team to ensure that each requirement is met.

Some common examples of insurance requirements are:

- Documentation of previous weight loss attempts and that non-surgical methods have been unsuccessful.

- Documentation that you meet the BMI qualification.

- Participation in an approved weight loss program (sometimes for as long as six months).

- Ruling out other causes of obesity, such as thyroid disease (Ensure you have bloodwork from your primary care provider showing normal thyroid function. If you are on medication for thyroid disease, the normal labs show that the disease is managed and not contributing to weight gain).

- Diagnostic imaging, EKG, cardiac stress test, pulmonary function tests, and a sleep apnea test.

- Participation in a comprehensive bariatric program, including nutrition evaluation and counseling, regular visits, and bariatric lifestyle education, including behavior change.

- Documentation of increased activity or exercise routine.

- A mental health or psychological evaluation.

- A letter of medical necessity from your bariatric surgeon.

- A complete evaluation from your primary care provider and specialists documenting the medical necessity and perceived benefits of bariatric surgery.

Usually, your surgeon will order the preoperative blood work, EKG, and chest x-ray just before surgery. So, you don't need to complete those at the beginning of the process—unless you see a specialist and they want to order tests. An EKG is typically accepted for six months after completion as long as it is normal. Your blood work will be analyzed closer to surgery for useful results. Finally, the chest x-ray can help rule out any undiagnosed concerns with your heart or lungs that may affect your surgery and recovery.

It is also helpful to communicate with your insurance company regularly. They may assign a nurse or specialist to your case, who you can check in with and update during the preparation process. If something seems off at any point, for example, something you were told on the phone conflicts with what you read on their website, get clarification.

Bariatric surgery policies can be complicated because it's considered an elective surgery. Even the insurance specialists who work for the company have a hard time understanding the criteria. So, **if you receive conflicting information, call back and talk to someone else until it makes sense, and get it in writing**. Also, involve the insurance coordinator on your bariatric team. They frequently have people they know and speak with at certain insurance companies. It will take you and your surgeon's insurance coordinator working together to successfully obtain your prior authorization.

If there are delays or you receive a denial, call your insurance company. Your bariatric insurance coordinator will do the same, but you have more influence as the customer. Again, work together—this is a complicated process. Denials are rare when insurance criteria have been met, but if you get one, there is usually an appeal process.

If you choose to appeal a denial, read the details and help your bariatric team with completing the paperwork. However, I always recommend you **do everything possible to ensure you meet your insurance criteria before a prior authorization is submitted**. Appeals can be challenging, and I would say about one in five are successful, based on my experience.

THE END IN SIGHT

Finally, when it comes to figuring out how much you will owe after insurance, that will depend on several items, such as your deductible and level of coverage. The hospital can help you determine an estimate. If you need help navigating insurance, I recommend the following website: .

It may feel like it's all uphill, but as you plan and work together with the experts on your bariatric team, you can achieve your coverage requirements. Receiving your insurance prior authorization for weight loss surgery coverage can feel like you just climbed a mountain and are finally enjoying your view from the top!

To help you get there, let's next discuss the importance of building an amazing team for your weight loss surgery transformation.

Chapter 6

Talking to Your Doctors & Choosing Your Surgeon

Alone, we can do so little; together we can do so much.
— Helen Keller

Kevin had no idea where to begin. As a hard-working father of three, he was still having a hard time wrapping his head around the fact that he needed to do something about his weight, let alone the idea of surgery.

At his annual physical, his doctor told him, "I understand that as a former athlete, you feel like a health-conscious individual, but your activity level and eating habits changed after high school. Unfortunately, your gradual weight gain over the last several years is affecting your health, and your efforts to lose weight have been unsuccessful. You are pre-diabetic, and your hemoglobin A1c continues to climb. Due to your family history, you are already at risk for heart disease, and your weight compounds that risk."

"What are you saying?" Kevin asked. The alarm was visible in his eyes.

"I'm going to refer you to the bariatric program for consideration of surgical weight loss. And I want you to approach it with an open mind," he responded with a tone of seriousness that Kevin suspected was reserved for conversations with an added element of gravity.

"Surgery? Like stapling my stomach?" Kevin said in disbelief.

"Dr. Stowe will explain the benefits and risks, as well as the details of the procedures she offers. I think you'll be surprised to learn what bariatric surgery entails, and I believe you are a good candidate. You should hear from a member of her team within a few days."

Kevin wondered how he got to this point, but he respected his physician's opinion. He decided to approach the idea with an open mind, as encouraged. Maybe there was something he didn't know. After all, he had never taken the time to learn about bariatric surgery as an option in his weight loss efforts. It seemed so extreme.

Likewise, the effects of diabetes and heart disease were an extreme consideration. He didn't want his family to suffer from his declining health or, worse, his premature death.

His thoughts swirled like a whirlwind as he solemnly drove home from the appointment. The next day, he decided it was time to continue the conversation by meeting with the local bariatric surgeon and talking to his wife.

It can be sobering to start a conversation with your care providers and those closest to you regarding weight loss surgery. I hope this chapter will help you understand the importance of having a **team approach and good communication** throughout the weight loss process.

PRIMARY CARE

Why do you need to talk to your regular doctor about having weight loss surgery? Your primary care provider (PCP) or general practitioner (GP) is a key member of your weight loss team.

They can advise you regarding lifestyle changes, diet and exercise programs, and weight loss medications if appropriate. Your primary care provider will also have documented your struggles and previous weight loss attempts, which will help determine medical necessity for your surgery.

Set up an appointment with your PCP the moment you start seriously considering weight loss surgery so they can guide and advocate for you. They know you and your health history better than any provider, so their direction is valuable to you and your bariatric team.

If you don't have a primary care provider, now is the time to get one. Ask around for recommendations, or sometimes I like to go to whoever is new. They have fresh perspectives and may be easier to schedule timely appointments with.

SPECIALISTS

Consider setting up appointments with any specialists you see, such as a cardiologist, pulmonologist, endocrinologist, etc. Your surgeon will want to know that they support you if you decide to pursue weight loss surgery.

Later on, you will need to meet with your PCP and specialists to **set up a post-surgical plan regarding treatment and medication changes within the days and weeks surrounding surgery**. You can discuss this initially and then call once you have your surgery date to schedule additional appointments.

Meeting with your specialists before surgery regarding blood pressure and blood glucose levels is of vital importance. Your readings for those levels will be significantly lower after surgery. The medications you take for high blood pressure, diabetes, and possibly others will need to be adjusted, or you may end up in a low range with potentially dangerous symptoms.

Your bariatric surgeon will include these considerations in their plan, and a physician will address them before you leave the hospital. But you still want to have a strategy in place with your specialized doctors before and after surgery to direct your care. The physician who manages each of your health conditions should be involved in your bariatric journey.

YOUR BARIATRIC TEAM & FACILITY

Every bariatric program should include a comprehensive, multidisciplinary team, meaning all the necessary professionals are involved. Your bariatric team will consist of your surgeon or team of surgeons and sometimes mid-level care providers, such as specialized physician assistants or nurse practitioners. It should also include bariatric-trained mental health providers, dieticians, nurses, and aides.

Hospital specialties, such as cardiology and pulmonology, may also be involved. Your team should have a bariatric coordinator and a staff member designated to handle insurance details. And don't forget your scheduling coordinator or front desk personnel—they can answer many of your questions or direct you to the right person to do so.

There are many considerations when choosing your bariatric team and facility (where your surgeon operates). Having surgery close to home has its advantages when you consider long-term follow-up and support.

If you must travel to your bariatric surgeon for financial, insurance, or other reasons, please **notify your surgeon's team right away that you are traveling so they can accommodate you as best they can**.

Many insurance policies require that you have surgery at a Center of Excellence or facility certified for bariatric surgery, such as a Blue Distinction Center for Blue Cross Blue Shield. Some smaller hospitals will never qualify for these designations because they require a higher patient flow than they can generate. As long as facilities meet all the other requirements for accreditation, safety, and equipment, there is nothing wrong with a hospital not being a Center of Excellence.

Your local hospital may be your easiest and best option. One perk of smaller hospitals, if they have good reviews and meet safety and performance measures, is that you receive more personalized care. You are not just a name or a case number. Your local surgeon cares about their community and those in it. They truly want you to succeed.

Some patients do require a higher level of care that smaller hospitals may not be able to provide, such as a high-level cardiac unit. Choose the hospital that is right for you. Your primary care doctor can help you determine which level of care you will need.

Finally, the bariatric coordinator is the person you can turn to for help with staying on track throughout the preoperative phase. They will be tracking your progress, so if you are lost at any point, reach out to them for direction.

It is so important that you **keep regular appointments** and communication with your bariatric team for a smooth process. It will initially feel overwhelming, but they have been doing this for a long time and know how to guide you. Trust them and the process they have put together for you, but don't hesitate to reach out for answers to your questions along the way.

SUPPORT

Aid, assistance, backing, encouragement, loyalty, protection, and relief are all words belonging to the same word family as support. Similarly, your support system consists of people in your life who can fill those roles—your family and friends, bariatric team, care providers, mental health counselors, bariatric support groups, and mentors. These are the people you thoughtfully choose to involve in your journey for support and guidance. They are invaluable.

Choosing a mentor can help pave the path to achieving your goals. A good mentor is someone who has had bariatric surgery and is committed to long-term success. You could speak to someone in a support group or a friend or family member who had weight loss surgery about mentoring you.

Some bariatric programs have a mentoring program and will recommend a mentor for you. Your mentor provides direction, encouragement, and constructive feedback, helping you navigate challenges. Likewise, they provide increased accountability and inspiration as you close the gap between their success and your own.

Crucial to your success, a proper support system will cheer you on when you succeed, offer a listening ear when you need to vent, and provide a fresh perspective when you face obstacles. Remember that as you **teach them about your bariatric lifestyle and encourage them to make changes with you**, they can boost your confidence and remind you that you're not alone. We are always better together.

After you sort out qualifying, insurance, and choosing your surgical team, you will start receiving a lot more personalized guidance from that team. You don't have to do it on your own. But knowing what to expect from the preoperative process can save you some agony because, again, it's a lot. The next chapter will provide a step-by-step list of the general bariatric process.

Chapter 7

Mapping It Out: The Bariatric Process

Give me six hours to chop down a tree, and I will spend the first four sharpening the axe.

— Abraham Lincoln

Young, beautiful, and in the process of a divorce, Jennifer came to our program seeking surgery as quickly as possible. She was ready to start her new life. She had done her research, probably twice over. When we discussed some of the appointments and tasks she would need to complete before coming in for her pre-surgery consultation with the surgeon, Jennifer proudly responded, "Done... I did that... Oh, I saw them already—I have the progress note." It was nice to have such a proactive patient, making our jobs easy.

The only problem with her being two steps ahead was that she felt like she was ready. However, she still had at least three months to prepare with our surgeon, dietician, and mental health counselor. No matter how much she read online or studied, she still needed **personalized guidance** from her surgical team.

Now, having worked as a clinical coordinator in addition to my nursing and coaching roles on bariatric teams, I would like to provide you with a good overview of what to expect during your bariatric process. But just as with any major journey, you need to stay flexible and open to personalized guidance. There isn't a one-size-fits-all trajectory when it comes to bariatric surgery.

Depending on your personal circumstances, there may be starts and stops along the way.

As you work together with your bariatric team, it may be determined that things need to be added, taken away, or moved around to arrive safely at your destination. There are many moving parts, and your team will do their best to help you navigate. You may receive an outline, checklist, or plan, but **please don't look at the steps simply as something to check off**—each one is vital to your success.

As a nurse, I feel I must include some additional helpful tidbits that can prevent complications. So, bear with me; it will all make sense at some point. Focus on the bolded steps, but please review the details as you get closer to your surgery. You are on a path that will forever change you. Immerse yourself in each step, and don't rush to the next in order to ensure you are truly prepared mentally and physically.

1—Talk to your primary care and specialized physicians for guidance and support. Obtain copies of the progress notes from these appointments so your bariatric team can see that these providers are aware of and support your decision to have bariatric surgery.

2—Determine how you will pay. Check your insurance to find out if you have coverage; if you do, get it in writing. If not, look into the possibility of using a health savings account, flexible spending account, or health reimbursement account (HSA, FSA, or HRA) that may be provided through your health insurance company. If you or your company have made contributions to one of those accounts, you may be able to apply it to surgery costs. Also, your chosen facility may offer payment programs or special financing options.

3—Choose your surgeon and facility. Remember to check your insurance requirements and weigh out the pros and cons of having surgery close to home or traveling for your surgery, as discussed in Chapters 4 through 6. Likewise, you will want to ensure that your bariatric surgeon is an "in-network" provider.

4—Have your primary care provider (PCP) send a referral to the surgeon's office. It is beneficial to the surgeon's team if they have a referral to review before you start the bariatric program. That way, they can put you in their tracking system and utilize information in the referral to help ensure you qualify for surgery.

MAPPING IT OUT: THE BARIATRIC PROCESS

If your PCP recommends a surgeon other than the one you have chosen, have an open discussion about the pros and cons of the two different options. Ultimately, it is your decision where you have surgery, but your PCP's perspective should always be considered.

5—Contact your facility's program or register online. Most bariatric programs have an **orientation or information seminar** you must complete before coming in for the first time. The orientation will cover qualification for surgery, bariatric procedures, risks and benefits, lifestyle expectations, program components, and how to proceed. Be sure to watch the entire orientation and take notes.

Before COVID, we loved doing in-person orientations and meeting our future patients, but most orientations are now online as a video or live seminar. Some have returned to in-person presentations but will also remain online for convenience.

Typically, after you complete an orientation, a bariatric team member will reach out to you to schedule your first appointment. Or, at the end of the seminar, they will ask you to call the office if you are interested in scheduling. You can register for orientations or information seminars online through the hospital website, or you can call the number listed.

6—Attend your initial appointment with your surgeon. You made it! You are finally meeting with a surgeon to discuss bariatric surgery and the rest of your life! This is exciting for you, your surgeon, and your entire team. There is nothing more rewarding than helping patients transform. You may want to **bring your support person** (remember, some surgeons require this) and come with **questions** you have written down beforehand. You should leave this appointment with a clear understanding of your preoperative process, including nutrition and mental health visits, and what you need to do to meet your insurance requirements.

Your surgeon will have specific lifestyle changes they want you to start focusing on, such as **eating small meals and snacks, eating out less, eating more protein, increasing activity, quitting smoking, and eliminating empty-calorie foods in the house**. As previously discussed, if you can, bring a list of diet and exercise changes that you have already started working on.

Surgeons love this because it demonstrates your commitment and readiness for change.

You will also receive a **handbook, manual, or guide**—sometimes online. Remember to read it, write down questions, and read it again. Highlight and tab sections that you want to stand out. The manual or guide provided will help you know where you are in your bariatric process and **what to expect next**. Don't get overwhelmed. Take it one step at a time and reach out to your team for additional direction when needed.

Surgery is not typically scheduled at the first appointment with your surgeon since there is a process to complete before surgery. As previously mentioned, it is not uncommon for patients to spend three to six months preparing for surgery after starting a bariatric program here in the US. You may find some "accelerated" programs here or abroad, but please ensure they still require all of the preoperative evaluations and education, as well as postoperative follow-up care. If they don't, run.

And just to clarify, when you start a bariatric program, that is *your* surgeon's or group of surgeons' program, and it is usually attached to the facility or hospital where your surgeon performs procedures. If you switch to a different bariatric program for some reason, like if you move, you will be starting over with a new surgeon and team.

7—Set up and attend initial appointments or classes with dieticians or nutritionists, mental health providers, nurses, mid-level practitioners, etc. Be sure to schedule your initial appointments or classes for nutrition as soon as you can. This is the **official start** of your bariatric lifestyle education process, so if your insurance has a time requirement for this aspect, delays with these appointments may push out your surgery date.

8—Follow up with your primary care provider and specialists and complete the tests they have ordered. Every time you leave a doctor's office, you should have a plan. A plan for when they would like to see you again, symptoms or problems you should report to them, or tests they would like you to complete. If you are unclear on what the plan is, please ask the doctor or a nurse so you are all on the same page.

9—Follow up with your bariatric team. Depending on your individual needs and your chosen bariatric program, you may see your surgeon only once or up to three or four times before surgery. Again, be sure you are clear on what the plan is, as well as the steps you should take in between visits to meet with additional providers or members of your team.

10—Complete your requirements. These are the steps that your surgeon and insurance policy require you to meet before surgery. They will consist of your bariatric lifestyle changes and education, nutrition appointments, mental health evaluation (and follow-up if necessary), diagnostic tests, and health care appointments.

It can be hard to navigate all of the different appointments. The more you can plan ahead and give yourself plenty of time to find child care or take time off of work, the better. Some appointments or classes may be offered in the evening or virtually, but for the most part, they will be during business hours. Please plan accordingly.

11—Meet with your surgeon for pre-surgery evaluation. This is it! It will feel surreal when you have completed the requirements and are ready to meet with your surgeon for your final pre-surgery discussion. Again, **bring your support person** to help sort out instructions and ask questions. This will be an in-depth discussion of the risks and benefits of your procedure, as well as your preparation and commitment to the bariatric lifestyle. You will be provided with instructions regarding surgery and given a **tentative surgical date**. Your surgery date may be around four weeks later, as it takes time to submit and receive the **insurance prior authorization**.

12—Complete pre-op shopping. Let's go shopping! You may have already purchased different shakes, vitamins, and postoperative diet options, but now is the time to make sure you have variety. At this point, you will have clearly outlined the stages of your pre-op and postoperative diet. Consider that your tastes may change after surgery, so don't buy cases of products but small quantities of **different options** to try. You will be surprised what your stomach and taste buds decide they do and do not like after surgery.

Your nutrition team will have suggestions for the best protein shakes. It is vital that you work consistently on meeting fluid and protein intake goals after surgery. Protein water (I know it sounds gross, but it's not) is also a great way to meet protein and hydration goals. If you are having difficulty finding these items in your local stores, you can order them online at sites like Amazon.

In grocery stores, there are three places to look for shakes and protein water. The first is near the pharmacy. This is usually the largest section. Then, you may find more options in the section with sports drinks, like Gatorade, Powerade, and Body Armor—grab a few of those while you're there (sugar-free). The last place to look is in the breakfast section, where you will find options like Carnation Instant Breakfast shakes or packets. Make sure to buy the versions that your bariatric team has recommended, such as "high protein," "low-sugar," or "light."

You will also have a list of clear liquid options, such as broth, sugar-free electrolyte drinks, certain juices, and sugar-free Jell-O. Be sure you don't buy items with fruit pulp, caffeine, or added sugar. Sugar-free popsicles are a great option as well. I will caution you that sugar alcohols used as artificial sweeteners (sorbitol, mannitol, xylitol, maltitol, etc.) can cause diarrhea if not used in moderation. Additionally, there is still a lot of controversy regarding the safety of artificial sweeteners in general and the effects of long-term, regular use. Please use them in moderation.

When you start adding soups and soft items, you may want to order some bariatric-specific items online. They often have added protein. Follow instructions closely, as eating the wrong textures too early will lead to gastrointestinal distress. Your stomach is still swollen and healing—be kind to it. Blending, pureeing, thinning, and diluting foods with water, milk, or broth early on can make all the difference.

Shopping for over-the-counter (OTC) medications and picking up prescriptions is also essential. **Some of your medications may need to be switched to liquid or chewable versions as recommended by your surgeon and providers to prevent swallowing difficulty.**

This is where discussing medication changes in detail before surgery can be so helpful, as Dani shared in a support group. She struggled to find one of her medications in liquid form before surgery and spent a good chunk of money to get it. Yet, after surgery, she no longer needed the prescribed medication due to rapid improvements in her health and was out over a hundred dollars. That was a hard pill to swallow! (Another bad joke).

I highly recommend buying some Miralax (the generic version is fine), Gas-X (simethicone) liquid or chewable, and liquid or chewable extra-strength

MAPPING IT OUT: THE BARIATRIC PROCESS

Tylenol (acetaminophen) to have on hand. Your team will advise you on using them if and when you need them.

The good news is pain management has improved by leaps and bounds. Some patients don't need more than extra-strength Tylenol at home after having an anesthetic pain pump placed in the operating room (your surgeon will explain options). This type of pain pump minimizes or eliminates the need for narcotic or opioid pain medication after surgery, which is significant, as the side effects of opioids can lead to complications.

13—Complete preoperative testing and hospital pre-anesthesia appointment.

Your hospital facility will schedule you for preoperative blood work and possible EKG and chest x-rays. At your pre-anesthesia appointment, they will have additional instructions to go over with you pertaining to the night before and the day of surgery. Please follow these closely. There is a **specific timeframe** that the hospital and your surgeon need tests completed before surgery, so bear in mind that if you have to reschedule this appointment, your surgery may also have to be rescheduled.

14—Follow your pre-op diet. The goal is not to starve you before surgery but primarily to reduce the size of your liver, which helps **lower your surgical risk**.[14] Following your pre-op diet is vital, but if something complicates this, reach out to your surgeon's office for direction. There are always options.

15—Surgery!!! Okay, this is *really* it. Before the operation, your **surgeon will come and talk to you to answer any last-minute questions**. Remember, nervouscited (nervous but excited) is normal! It has not been easy getting to this point, but you did it!

After surgery, most patients stay in the hospital for one night. There are surgeons who perform outpatient or "same-day" sleeve and bypass procedures. As a nurse, I would not want my loved one going home on the day of surgery since postoperative monitoring is crucial for patients, and the ASMBS still recommends a one to two-night stay.[15] You should be monitored to ensure your vital signs are stable and you will be able to drink enough water to stay hydrated after going home.

Please get up and **walk** around regularly in the hospital and after you go home. Walking helps prevent blood clots and pneumonia, speeds up healing, and aids **pain management**, even though it may not feel that way initially.

Be sure your pain is managed before you get up to walk around, but do not take pain medication shortly before getting up; you may be dizzy or light-headed at first. Sit up slowly and move to the side of the bed, where you should wait a moment for your blood pressure to equalize before standing. Doing so will help prevent orthostatic hypotension, which is low blood pressure resulting from getting up too quickly and can cause you to pass out. Your nurses will guide you on positioning yourself in and out of bed.

Ice packs can also be very effective after surgery. If one is not provided, don't hesitate to ask for one. An ice pack will help manage postoperative swelling and pain. Just be sure you aren't overdoing it and preventing adequate circulation to the healing incisions with too much cold temperature. Your surgical team will advise you on how to use ice packs after surgery.

There is one last detail that I can't leave out. An **incentive spirometer** is an essential item you will start using in the hospital. You may have seen or used one before. It is a clear plastic apparatus that has a wide, flexible straw coming off of it. The incentive spirometer helps with lung inflation to prevent complications like pneumonia and respiratory depression after surgery. You will inhale or suck into the straw to expand your lungs.

It also has an interesting effect on inflammation. Patients often call the office a day or two after going home from the hospital to report a low-grade fever (less than 100.4) and concerns about an infection. This low fever can be a normal part of the inflammatory effects of surgery, and using your incentive spirometer

MAPPING IT OUT: THE BARIATRIC PROCESS

as directed can resolve it. Of course, if you have a true fever, it won't work, and you will need to call your surgeon's office immediately or go to the emergency department for evaluation.

The hospital and your bariatric team will have instructed you on problems to watch for after surgery. Don't hesitate to call if you are unsure. It is always better to be safe.

16—Come home, WALK, manage pain, use your incentive spirometer, and follow diet stages closely. Did I mention you should walk? Remember, walking helps prevent blood clots, improves healing with better circulation, and decreases pain. Don't overdo it, but please get up and walk around at least every two hours while awake. Do a little more each time.

17—Follow up with your surgeon and bariatric team as planned, including your PCP and specialists. Complete blood work as ordered.

18—Recover and progress. Continue to practice your bariatric lifestyle habits, advance your diet as outlined, and **establish new routines** as advised by your bariatric team.

19—Stay on the path and enjoy the benefits! Attend support groups, monitor your progress, and stay accountable.

20—Complete ongoing follow-up and reach out with questions or concerns! Your surgeon will instruct you regarding any concerns you should contact the office with. Still, if you feel something is a problem, or you have a minor problem that is getting worse, you should always contact your surgeon. If a problem is unrelated to the surgery or you aren't sure, contact your primary care provider.

I know that was a lot of information. But hopefully, it gives you a better idea of what to expect. You might feel you should tackle it now and start checking off as many things as possible, but please don't hurry. From my experience, most patients who are in a rush and aren't **fully engaged in each step of the process** tend to struggle postoperatively.

Learning to swim after you're already in the deep end is hard! Don't just get your toes wet. Dive in now and immerse yourself in *your* bariatric journey to glide to the finish line. And when things get tough, which they will, take Dory's advice from *Finding Nemo* and, "Just keep swimming, just keep swimming, just keep swimming, swimming, swimming."

In the next section, I hope to provide some inspiration to help fuel you to persevere through the challenging times.

Part 3: INSPIRATION

Early in my bariatric career, I had the pleasure of working with a tough-as-nails, beautiful young woman whose life had been difficult. In her twenty-one years, Kelsey experienced abuse, bullying, and discrimination. In response, she had developed a solid outer persona. She sent a "don't mess with me" message with her piercings, tattoos, favorite black hoodie, and strong posture—but she was sweet as could be. She made the decision to have weight loss surgery after battling with polycystic ovary syndrome (PCOS) and its miserable symptoms. If you have PCOS, you know what I'm talking about.

Her insurance required her to lose a certain percentage of body weight before surgery, as used to be common until research demonstrated that there was little to no benefit to doing so. We worked on diet and exercise changes for almost a year with some progress, but not enough. She ultimately decided to take a break and moved away for a fresh start.

Months later, I emailed Kelsey and asked her how she was doing. For some reason, I asked her if she had stepped on the scale lately. Sometimes, stepping back from a stressful situation makes all the difference in weight loss plateaus. She responded and said she would weigh herself. To her amazement, she had lost the required weight without knowing it. She was ecstatic and wanted to start making preparations for surgery.

Kelsey did very well after surgery. Not to say that she didn't have ups and downs, but her weight loss results were incredible. She enjoyed staying active and followed her diet guidelines diligently.

About one year after surgery, she and her boyfriend were in a horrific accident. Kelsey was thrown from the vehicle and suffered a terrible spinal injury, among other serious injuries. It seemed like she was in the hospital for a lifetime, but as she endured her hospitalization, surgical spinal repair, and recovery, she found new strength. She told me that one of the surgeons explained that if she had not had bariatric surgery and lost fifty percent of her body weight, she would not have survived the accident. This news was eye-opening to us both.

Over the years, I have continued to observe this young lady, who became dear to me, endure tragedy after tragedy—some of which are too heartbreaking to mention. However, she keeps getting back up. She keeps living and loving, true to herself. I only hope she knows how courageous, strong, and beautiful she is; she must know she has a purpose. Her strength, resilience, and determination have been inspiring. I love you, Kelsey.

There is no explanation for why Kelsey has endured so much, both pre- and postoperatively, but I hope sharing her story inspires you with her strength and determination.

By now, you have a good understanding of how to get started on your journey physically. Let's switch gears and get to the **heart** of why you are reading this book.

Clearly, if you are considering weight loss surgery, you are seeking change. So where do you begin? You start right here by **switching your focus** from the problem to the solution. But first, we have to figure out what drives us. Why are you inspired to change? In Chapter 8, I will share a powerful tool. Then, in Chapter 9, we will complete an exercise to make that shift from problem to solution. This next section will be short but sweet!

Chapter 8

Find Your Why

Sow a thought and you reap an action,
Sow an act and you reap a habit,
Sow a habit and you reap a character,
Sow a character and you reap a destiny.

— Ralph Waldo Emerson

Have you really thought about *why* you are considering or had weight loss surgery? Many people think they have but might realize later their decision was based on surface-level thoughts or reactions.

The more *meaning and feeling* we attach to a change we are making, the more likely we are to stick with it. **When our purpose is rooted deeply, we let nothing get in our way.** That is the reason I recommend the Seven Levels Deep exercise.

I learned this powerful tool from *New York Times* best-selling author, self-help expert, and entrepreneur Dean Graziosi. The objective is to keep asking yourself why you want or need to do something until you get to the **heart and soul of your driving force.** You will ask yourself "why" seven times—each time digging deeper for the true meaning in your motivation to create change.

Finding your why is about aligning your actions with your values and passions to create a meaningful and fulfilling life. Once you find your why, you can return to it as often as needed for feelings of strength, inspiration, and guidance.

I love Dean Graziosi's example. He shared his life-changing experience with this exercise on his website:

> *If you asked a million people, "Would you like to make more money?" Everybody would answer yes. But you probably already know that only a small group are actually willing to work for it. So the next most important question is "WHY are you willing to work for it?"*
>
> *Maybe you think that's easy to answer... I used to think that. But a friend took me through an exercise that changed my life forever...He asked me this one simple question... "Why would someone pay you 10 grand to help them get more success?" And I answered with something like... "I've been through this experience and I know they can do it. If they would just apply themselves more." He was like, "Well, why is it important they apply themselves more?"*
>
> *I said something about wanting to raise the standards in the self-education industry. And how I wanted other people in this space to step up or step out. He told me that was all great, but it was coming from my head. He pushed me harder and asked, "But why is stepping up or stepping out important, Dean?"*
> *Still coming from my head I said, "I want to leave a legacy for my family." He asked me three more times, rephrasing the question with my answer to the previous question.*
>
> *I admit it – I was getting more than frustrated! So I just said the first thing on my heart... "I never wanna go backwards!"*
>
> *And at that moment, I thought about my past... living in a trailer park, living in a bathroom, having no lunch money, my parents fighting over money and all those painful memories... That was it, I thought. "Because I'm never going backwards. No way!"*
>
> *And all of a sudden my physiology changed. I had got it into my heart. I was like, "Oh [wow], I feel this." But I made the mistake of thinking we were done... Then he said to me, "Dean, why is it*

> *important to not go backwards?"*
>
> *Immediately I thought about my kids. And I started crying. Not like small tears, like ugly crying. And my staff was around! I was so embarrassed...But I had found my real "why" when I finally choked out, "I want my kids to have choices." And I could see their faces and could only think about them. And I realized, "I got it." I got my why.*
>
> *If you can dig into your heart and answer why you want it from this emotional space, then nothing gets in your way...*
>
> *No matter how tough things get or what obstacles come up that get in your way...*
>
> *Chances are you're going to succeed because nobody can stop you once you know your "why". So dig into your heart. Find your why. And don't let anybody get in your way.*[16]

I know it may sound simple, but try it. If you don't find profound meaning in your why the first time, try it again. Remember to answer from your heart and not your head. Yours might start like this: Why am I considering weight loss surgery? I want to lose weight and feel better. Why do I want to lose weight and feel better? And so on. Each "why" question is based on your answer to the previous question.

As you complete the exercise, keep the following questions in mind:

1. What activities genuinely excite and energize you; what are your passions?
2. What core values and beliefs guide your decision-making?
3. What past experiences have brought you joy, fulfillment, or a sense of accomplishment?
4. What problems do you feel passionate about solving; what impact do you want to have on the world?

After considering these questions, I hope you will use the tool I have provided to find your why. Complete it here, but you also may want to keep it in your phone and journal. Put it on a sticky note on the mirror or whatever keeps it at the forefront of your thoughts. Stay open-minded and be patient. It may take some time, but once you find your why, you will change.

This exercise is one of the most important steps to **create lasting change**. Why? Because it provides us with a clear purpose, helping us **turn in the right direction and away from things in our lives that do not serve us**. I say this with conviction because it helped me, and I know it can help you.

Finding Your Why—Seven Levels Deep

Level 1: **What do you want to do?**

_____

_____

Level 2: **Why is that important to you?** (From your previous answer)

_____

_____

Level 3: **Why is that important to you?**

_____

_____

Level 4: **Why is that important to you?**

_____

_____

Level 5: **Why is that important to you?**

_____

_____

Keep going—you're almost there!

Level 6: **Why is that important to you?**

_____

_____

Level 7: **And why is _that_ important to you?**

_____

_____THIS IS YOUR WHY!

I hope this exercise was helpful to you. If you're like me and Dean Graziosi, you might be a little emotional right now. **It will be different this time** because your why is bigger than you. Your why likely involves people you love and who depend on you, or it involves the future that you refuse to see slip away. Your "why" should make you feel unstoppable because it means more than anything.

Regarding her why, a sixty-nine-year-old patient said, "I knew if I didn't have the surgery, I would be dead soon." She refused to leave her family prematurely. They need and love her, and she loves them too much not to change. Now, six months post-op, she has achieved her weight loss goal sooner than expected and no longer needs handfuls of medications daily. She is overjoyed at her success.

***

Now that you know your deep-rooted **why**, we must figure out **exactly what**. What will this change include, and who do you want to be?

Chapter 9

Create Your Success Mindset

Talk to yourself the way you would to someone you love.
— Brené Brown

Ann worked in the hospital as a head respiratory therapist and was respected for her clinical and leadership skills. I had always enjoyed working with her on med/surg and was excited when she joined our bariatric program to pursue weight loss surgery.

As a new professional in the medical field, I looked up to Ann, so I was surprised when such a seemingly confident and competent clinician confided in me that she had low self-esteem and didn't like who she was. I shared with Ann that I admired her and encouraged her to give herself compassion as we started setting goals and working on lifestyle changes.

Shortly after we began our one-on-one bariatric coaching together, I passed her in the hall outside the breakroom in the hospital. I had given in to temptation and had a cupcake in my hand.

I was so embarrassed that I, the person coaching Ann to stay away from excess sugar, was caught red-handed—I am human, too! My knee-jerk reaction was to say, "Shhhhhhhh" as I put my finger to my lips, like, "Don't tell anyone the bariatric nurse is eating a cupcake!" I was sure my embarrassment was all over my face—but evidently, I was wrong.

Ann had taken my gesture differently. As a result of my insensitivity and her self-consciousness, she interpreted the interaction as if I was expressing that she was *not allowed* to eat a cupcake because she was suffering from obesity and preparing for weight loss surgery. I discovered my miscommunication after our surgeon called me into his office and expressed his disappointment in me.

The incident had gone all the way to hospital administration after Ann had shared with a coworker how I hurt her. I was mortified. I love and respect my patients and would NEVER intend to cause them distress or pain. I explained the situation to my boss and assured him I would make it right.

That night, I spent thirty or forty minutes explaining myself to Ann and trying to reassure her. But no matter how I approached it, I wasn't able to do so. I was heartbroken. She continued to attend her appointments with me, but it was never the same—she completed her preparations quickly and efficiently but remained guarded with me.

Months after surgery, Ann shared in our support group that she continued to struggle with her self-image and was slowly gaining some weight back. It wasn't until she moved away and met her future husband that she finally transformed. At follow-up appointments, we could see that Ann was happy, healthy, and confident. She was finally the incredible person we knew, yet it took her a little longer to see.

It is with sadness that I suspect Ann previously told herself for years, maybe decades, that she was not enough. The negative thoughts likely flooded her mind when she looked in the mirror disapprovingly. Just as most of us are prone to at times, Ann subconsciously attached those thoughts to interactions, giving them painful meanings—interactions such as the one she and I had in the hallway of the hospital.

I didn't know Ann's life story and why she struggled with self-esteem, but I learned a powerful lesson about sensitivity and empathy through the experience with the cupcake. You never know what kind of internal language someone uses with themselves. They may seem confident and capable on the outside, but they may be swimming in doubt on the inside.

Ann deserved better from me. I made a mistake. However, I learned how my own insecurities about practicing what I preach could interfere with my ability

CREATE YOUR SUCCESS MINDSET

to properly show up and care for my patients. I believe we can all work on our internal language to show better compassion for ourselves and others.

REWRITE YOUR STORY

Have you ever paid attention to your conversation with yourself throughout the day? Often, we are subconsciously creating our own story or reality by telling ourselves the wrong things. Does any of this sound familiar? "What is wrong with me? I can't do that. I'm not like them. I'll never find the time. It's just not possible"—GUILTY! We all do it. But we must stop sabotaging ourselves.

The story we tell ourselves becomes our reality because it's what we focus on. Thoughts become things (actions or circumstances in our lives) because we base our decisions on them. If you want to change, tell yourself that you *can*, you *are*, and **it is possible**. It all begins with our thoughts.

I learned this very helpful exercise about changing your story[17] from the master of personal development, Tony Robbins. Like Dean Graziosi, Tony Robbins is also a #1 *New York Times* bestselling author, entrepreneur, philanthropist, and he is the nation's #1 life and business strategist. He offers incredible guidance and motivation through his website, YouTube videos, and free app called Breakthrough. I consider him an excellent resource when it comes to personal transformation.

Part of succeeding with weight loss surgery, weight loss, or any significant change in our lives involves changing the way we talk to ourselves and the story we tell ourselves. You can use this exercise in all areas of your life—health, finances, relationships, education, career, and personal growth.

So when you can, **sit down in a quiet space without distraction** and write down the *current* story you have been telling yourself about who you are. What kind of person are you? How do you live? What do you think people say about you? What do you say about yourself?

Now, **get rid of your old story**. Rip it up, crumple it, throw it away, burn it (safely), stomp on it, or pound it until it's unrecognizable. Please don't skip this step. Identifying the negative story you've been telling yourself about who you are will help you be specific about creating the person you want to become. We command our mind and our body with our self-talk. If our self-talk is negative, we are creating more negativity. If our self-talk is positive, we create positive momentum.

Next, **rewrite your story**. Who do you want to be? What does that look like? What do people say about you now? What actions are you taking? What meaning does it give to your life? Get as detailed as possible, including how you will feel each day as you achieve this new version of yourself.

Now, **change your inner dialogue to align with this story**. And when the negative self-talk creeps in, as it always does, push it out! Read your new story regularly, even say it out loud until you believe every word and know **you are becoming this person.**

My Story

This is your **what—the lasting change you will create**. Remember, always **come back to your why if you get lost**. I recommend starting a journal to record your thoughts and progress. Some nice bariatric-formatted journals are available online, or you can use your own. For now, tab or turn down these pages containing your **why** and **your story** so you can refer back to them frequently.

PERSONAL GROWTH

With your "why" and your new story in mind, let's take a closer look at behavior change. Specific steps will help ensure you succeed. We have already discussed how important it is to connect deeply to your desired outcome by attaching it to your feelings. To effectively transform, let's **combine the inspiration you have found through the self-help exercises with evidence-based behavior change techniques**[18] you will find throughout the remainder of this book. I will summarize these techniques for lasting change in the resources section at the end of the book.

FIND AWARENESS OF YOUR PATTERNS & TRIGGERS

As we reflect on who we are becoming, we will identify behaviors that don't align with the best version of ourselves, such as watching too much TV, eating fast food, or scrolling on our phones aimlessly—guilty again. Sometimes, behaviors and patterns are referred to as coping mechanisms; we use them to cope with past trauma, events, situations, or feelings that are uncomfortable or we may be trying to avoid.

There are healthy and unhealthy coping mechanisms. Substance abuse and food addiction are common examples of unhealthy coping mechanisms. Healthy coping mechanisms include listening to music, journaling, meditation, reading, hobbies, going for a walk, or talking to a trusted friend. To effectively help us, healthy coping mechanisms should provide a sense of fulfillment.

Food and substance abuse can stem from a lack of healthy coping mechanisms. If you are struggling with addiction and want to change, please know that it's okay to ask for help, and many resources are available to support you. You don't have to face this alone. Start with turning to someone you can trust, like a family member, friend, or healthcare professional. With guidance and encouragement, you can take steps in a new direction. Remember, seeking help is not a sign of weakness but of strength. It shows you're willing to take control of your life and make positive changes. I believe in you and your ability to overcome addiction.

When it comes to changing patterns that don't align with who we want to be, these are the **behaviors that we constantly tell ourselves we need to improve** upon as we are doing them. So how do we change?

Change involves an honest and sometimes uncomfortable look inward. Note some of the unhealthy patterns you may be participating in. Then, think about what triggers you to do them. A trigger can be specific thoughts, people, memories, places, or situations you find yourself in. If you can identify your triggers and work on eliminating some of those, such as not passing your favorite fast-food place on your way home from work when you are tired and starving, you can interrupt the pattern.

Replacing old behaviors with new ones can help fill the void. For example, bring a healthy, balanced snack to work that you can have between lunch and dinner—curb your hunger, so you aren't tempted by the colorful lit-up signs and window-sized fast-food images on your drive home. You can also interrupt behaviors with distraction, such as a hobby, reading, or calling a friend. Let's get specific and write some things down to get started:

BEHAVIOR PATTERN	TRIGGER	REPLACE/INTERRUPT WITH

This exercise may feel oversimplified for some behaviors that are programmed deep within us. Consequently, the help of a mental health professional is invaluable. Identifying and working on our unhealthy behavior patterns is a vital step for lasting change. It's not easy, but the battle will be worth it if you want to get unstuck from within harmful patterns that affect you and possibly your loved ones.

Journaling and seeking feedback are additional ways to work on your patterns. Set aside regular time for self-reflection through journaling. Write about your experiences, thoughts, and emotions. Look for recurring themes, triggers, and patterns in your writing. Don't forget to reflect on past experiences and ask trusted friends, family members, or mentors for their observations and feedback. Sometimes, others can see patterns in our behavior that we may overlook ourselves.

Please be patient with yourself and your body. Our goal is **progress, not perfection.** Just keep moving in the right direction, and when things don't go as planned, **brush it off and keep going**.

BECOME MORE MINDFUL

Mindfulness can help us stay present, calm, and more self-aware. If you're like me, finding some calm after thinking about behavior patterns I need to work on sounds great. Let's start by taking three slow, deep breaths, in through your nose and out through your mouth.

Great. To develop the practice of mindfulness, start by finding a quiet, peaceful, comfortable space. Sit or lie down and pay attention to your body and your surroundings. Notice how your body feels? What is your breathing doing? What do you hear? Look around at everything and really notice it. Or you can close your eyes… What are you thinking? How are you feeling at that moment? Stay present, **simply observe**, and try to practice being nonjudgmental. **Accept whatever arises without labeling it as good or bad.**

So, how does this relate? Try to notice the meaning that you attach to certain thoughts. For example, my six-year-old didn't listen to me when I asked her to pick up her toys. Therefore, she doesn't respect me—OR, is she tired and hungry, incapable of doing anything until her physical needs are met? We do this to ourselves, too. Does this sound familiar? I didn't accomplish what I wanted today, so I must be a failure. Wrong! It doesn't mean anything other than you get to keep trying.

Many people practice mindfulness in the context of meditation. You can also search for more specific mindfulness techniques online. Many apps centered on mental and physical health offer mindfulness exercises and tracking. You may already have one.

Even if it's just a few deep breaths, practicing being mindful can bring a sense of peace, acceptance, and focus to our day. Try being mindful while walking, eating, or spending time with family. Put down your phone and eliminate other distractions. You will experience additional benefits of reduced stress, improved mental clarity, and better emotional regulation, enhancing overall well-being and resilience to life's challenges.

Moving forward, I encourage you to become more mindful and practice positivity during reflection exercises. A positive attitude with self-awareness earned through identifying our unhealthy behavior and thought patterns can lead to healthier relationships, enhanced decision-making skills, increased empathy, and achievement.[19] It is a practice for refinement as we work lifelong to better ourselves.

**

Now, I hope you feel inspired by your new story and are ready to create a specific plan for developing healthier habits as you become more aware of your patterns. If you aren't yet, it's okay. There is more help available. It's alright to need more time. In fact, it's better, unless your health is in jeopardy, to take more time and make sure you're truly ready to commit to the bariatric lifestyle if it's right for you.

Figure out where you are ready to start making changes and get support through your bariatric team and personal support system. Utilize your behavioral or mental health counselor to help you with the challenging steps unique to you.

I encourage you to start setting specific goals as you continue modifying your behavior patterns. Aiming toward a goal will direct you. Remember, willpower alone will not get you there. Having a **positive inner dialogue** or self-talk, **taking action consistently**, and **keeping focus** by **surrounding yourself with those who are already successful** will keep you moving in the right direction.

Your purpose will be much clearer if you have found your why, rewritten your story, and developed increased self-awareness to create a success-driven mindset. That means it's time to take action. Let's get working on your transformation into the new you. In the next section, we will discuss where you can begin.

Part 4: ACTION

I'm reminded of two very different women when I think about patients making great efforts to change their lives. One was young and had most of her life ahead of her. She and her husband desperately wanted to start a family, but her weight was disrupting her fertility. The other had just begun her retirement and wanted to make the most of it by enjoying traveling and spending time with her family.

Both were up against serious challenges, between a history of abuse, physical and mental health struggles, and lack of extended family support. Despite their trials, these women have done incredibly well by working hard on themselves. They set goals, changed their thought and behavior patterns, and developed better habits. Both have exceeded their weight loss goals and kept the weight off successfully for nearly a decade.

What these women have in common is an incredible drive to succeed because they refuse to go back to their old ways of life. Each connected to their "why" and who they wanted to become. Each made **a decision** and a commitment to herself.

The Latin origin of the word "decision" means "to cut off." These two women cut off old habits, thought patterns, and unhealthy coping mechanisms. They immersed themselves in learning about bariatric surgery and what it takes to succeed. Each made changes to their lifestyle long before surgery and practiced bariatric habits. They took the time to learn helpful details, like avoiding carbonation or using portion containers to ensure their success.

Have they had times of self-doubt or struggle? Of course, they have! And they will have more, but their determination remains fixed. They continue to take action as best they can to move in the right direction. They learn from their mistakes, and they don't beat themselves up about not being perfect. Each woman keeps returning to her "why" and doesn't look back.

Chapter 10

Start Now, Here's How

They always say time changes things, but you actually have to change them yourself.
— Andy Warhol

Tiffanie was desperate to start losing weight. She felt sluggish and depressed, and her lower back hurt. At only thirty-nine, she wasn't willing to accept that this was how the rest of her life would play out.

We started making gradual changes to her diet and activity level, such as walking more and decreasing empty-calorie foods. She lost a pound or two, then would get off track and regain it.

I suggested that Tiffanie start tracking her food and activity on an app so she could see how the high-calorie foods she was consuming affected her daily calorie intake. Tiffanie tracked a little here and there for several weeks. I tried to help her understand the importance of tracking for a whole day at a time to see her daily energy balance, even if she didn't track every day.

The struggle continued for about three months. Then, finally, Tiffanie started tracking every day. When she saw the daily calorie balance between her activity and the foods she consumed, she was immediately motivated to practice more discipline. Within a week, she was down two pounds. The weight loss continued at about two pounds per week as she continued tracking her food and activity and achieved her goal of burning more calories than she consumed.

Tiffanie was amazed that committing to the process of tracking or self-monitoring could have such an impact. She could eventually go for days without tracking, even though she still followed her guidelines. The value of portion control and dining out less had become key to maintaining her weight loss.

When Tiffanie feels off track or starts to notice some regain, she goes right back to tracking her food and activity. It is a lifesaver for her and many others who may not be ready for surgery, who are preparing for surgery, or who have had surgery and may be struggling with regain.

MEASURE IT TO MANAGE IT

This is where I *really* get all health coachy on you. It's alright if you feel some apprehension. You don't have to change everything overnight. You don't even have to change *everything*. We just need to create enough momentum to keep you moving in the direction you want to go. I'm here to help! Let's start with a straightforward concept: **Measure it to manage it**. And by the way, when I talk about change, **we can *all* do better**, so please don't ever feel like I'm pointing a finger.

From here on out, look for the infinity heart symbol for the **family-friendly habits** you can begin implementing now with your support person and loved ones. If a lifestyle habit does not have this symbol, it is a bariatric-specific habit and should only be utilized by bariatric patients, *or* it is not appropriate for children.

SELF-MONITOR AND PLAN AHEAD

One of the most beneficial habits you can develop is self-monitoring using food, activity, and hydration tracking apps. Try notes on your smartphone or paper logs if you want to keep it simple. Doing so can help you **become aware of your eating and exercise patterns**. It will also empower you to better understand calorie and macronutrient breakdown so you can make better food choices.

Patients like Tiffanie often take months to start tracking consistently because it takes a lot of effort initially. Yet, upon doing so, they start seeing the benefits almost immediately (noticing trends and losing weight by being more self-aware). Estimating does not work. What if you hired someone to remodel your bathroom, and they didn't take a single measurement? It wouldn't work out very well, would it? We need current measurements to know how to change something. I have witnessed time and time again the correlation between successful long-term weight loss and using self-monitoring tools.

To be most effective, measure your **food and water intake, activity, body circumferences, weight, and take before and after photos**. I understand this may be troubling for many of you who are triggered negatively by the number on the scale, so I will offer alternatives. Trust me, you will want to have starting measurements and photos to track your progress. These are your bragging rights later on, and you will have earned them!

Research confirms that those who **use self-monitoring tools frequently and consistently** have greater long-term weight loss and maintenance success.[20, 21] The remaining headings in this chapter consist of each aspect you may include to self-monitor.

FOOD INTAKE

As a weight loss coach, I highly recommend downloading an app or using a website for food logging or nutrition tracking. Digital tracking does the math for you, so you know where you are and where you can improve.

I currently use My Fitness Pal, but I also like the Fitbit app, Samsung Health, and Lose It. I haven't tried others, such as Apple Health, Google Fit, Fooducate, and My Diet Coach. So, do a search and base your choice on what you may already have access to or what suits you best. There are also bariatric-specific apps, such as Baritastic.

After you download an app or create an account on a website, you will be asked to enter your height, weight, age, and gender. This is to determine your calorie and nutrition requirements.

You will also be prompted to enter a goal. Be careful because if you enter more than two pounds per week, you will likely end up on a very low-calorie diet (VLCD). A VLCD is less than 1200 calories per day and can lead to rapid weight loss, including significant muscle loss. Muscle loss will result in a slowed metabolism and eventual weight regain (the yo-yo effect), which I will explain more in the next chapter. One to two pounds per week is a healthy rate for sustainable weight loss.[22] Or you can choose to maintain your weight if your primary goal is to develop the habit of tracking. I do not recommend food logging and calorie counting for adolescents unless it is under the supervision of a physician.

You will notice that each day is broken down into meals and snacks as you log. For example,

breakfast, snack, lunch, snack, dinner, and possibly one last small protein-based snack (around 100 calories). This is commonly referred to as eating small, frequent meals. If you have kids, you are already used to pulling out snacks two or three times per day, so why not do the same for yourself? This is a great way to start eating smaller portions with meals because you won't be starving by the time you get to the next meal.

Logging or tracking your food intake is valuable for understanding calories and macronutrients. Fats, carbohydrates, and proteins are macronutrients. Carbohydrates and proteins contain four calories per gram—whereas fats contain nine calories per gram.[23] It takes more than twice as much energy to burn off a gram of fat as a carbohydrate or protein. We quickly learn the value of measuring and tracking our fat intake when we see its significant role in our daily calorie balance.

PROTEIN

Remember that protein indicates nourishment after surgery. **Adequate protein intake is vital for healthy tissues, including muscles. After surgery,**

it is crucial for healing and maintaining strength. If you are not eating enough protein after surgery, your body will break down muscle.

Blood tests for your prealbumin, albumin, and protein levels can indicate signs of malnutrition and are all related to your protein intake.[24] You will be required to eat sixty to one hundred grams of protein, as recommended by your surgeon.[25]

There are two types of protein—complete protein and incomplete protein. Complete protein comes mostly from animal sources, such as beef, poultry, pork, dairy, eggs, and fish. Quinoa, amaranth, and buckwheat are healthy grains that offer complete proteins. Whole sources of soy like tofu, tempeh, miso, and edamame also contain complete protein, as do chia seeds and pistachios. A protein is complete when it contains the nine essential amino acids (building blocks of protein) that our bodies can't produce on their own.

We get incomplete proteins from non-animal sources like nuts and seeds, beans, legumes, vegetables, and grains.[26] Remember that incomplete proteins often contain more carbohydrates or fats than protein. They are still good protein sources, but please don't ignore the fats or carbs they provide. If you are vegetarian or vegan, you are probably used to eating a variety of incomplete proteins to obtain complete protein in your diet.

Complete Proteins	Incomplete Proteins
Meat, eggs, fish, dairy, quinoa, amaranth, buckwheat, soy, hemp, chia seeds, pistachios	Beans, legumes, vegetables, most grains, nuts, and seeds

While complete proteins may sound like the ideal option, it's best to

practice eating a variety of proteins from complete and incomplete sources. Your dietician can help you personalize protein options based on your food preferences.

CALORIE BALANCE BEFORE SURGERY

Understanding your daily calorie balance is like having a power drill instead of a handheld screwdriver when it comes to your weight loss tools. You can lose weight without it. But, if you do monitor your calorie balance, it will significantly speed up your results.

As you may know, a calorie is a unit of energy. It's technically a kilocalorie (kcal), so if you see that abbreviation somewhere, it just means calories. Your tracking apps will use equations for calorie balance (**energy intake versus energy expenditure**) to determine whether you are losing or gaining weight.

What's more, you can

use a fitness tracker for more accuracy regarding how many calories you burn or your energy expenditure. This is determined by your activity and your resting metabolic rate (RMR) or basal metabolic rate (BMR). RMR and BMR are often used interchangeably and refer to how many calories it takes to keep your body alive if you were to rest all day.[27] You can use the tracker on your phone or your smartwatch, or you can purchase a cheap fitness tracker watch from Walmart or Amazon.

A fitness tracker calculates your energy expenditure (RMR + activity) based on your steps or movement it detects and your heart rate, in addition to your age, weight, height, and birth-assigned sex.

Many smartwatches sync with your food-logging app, like My Fitness Pal, or have options in their own apps (Fitbit, Samsung Health, etc.). So it can be fun to have estimations of your **calories in (food and drinks)** and **calories out (RMR + activity)** throughout the day to help you make food and activity choices.

When it comes to daily calorie balance, think ahead to keep your food and activity working together for you—eat for your activity level. If you are tired and sitting around after a long, hard day, you don't need a high-calorie dinner. Conversely, if you are going for a three-hour hike, you should probably eat a decent meal beforehand and bring a snack.

START NOW, HERE'S HOW

It's all about the big-picture perspective. Seeing that you only need 1,000 more steps to reach your goal or that rice and beans are waaaaaaaaaaay too many carbs can motivate you to do things differently—take that walk and skip the rice and beans!

Recall that your bariatric guidelines and stomach will determine how many calories you can eat *after* surgery. **You typically will not have a calorie goal after weight loss surgery.** Yet, suppose you start to experience some weight regain months or years after surgery. In that case, your dietician may recommend a calorie range.

We've covered a lot of ground, and you might think, "That's all great if you're a health coach or an athlete, but it's not for me." But it is for you! You can **learn to track and benefit for the rest of your life**.

Don't just take it from me—read the educational topics within your tracking website or app. They will explain how your goals and progress are calculated and provide tips for improvement. Understanding the basic math involved in nutrition and activity tracking can empower you to make more progress than ever before!

Remember, if we burn (RMR + activity) more calories than we consume (food and drinks), we should lose weight. Again, a calories in versus calories out approach is oversimplified. Many more factors contribute to weight gain and loss than eating and exercise. However, don't we want to acquire all the tools? Food and activity tracking is a good one that all adults can benefit from.

WATER

Drink some water. Yep, stop and drink some water—I just did. You already know how important it is to your health, but as a reminder, staying hydrated is vital for supporting digestion, transporting nutrients, cushioning joints, and flushing toxins from our bodies. It also helps with energy levels and cognitive function. So remember, when you are tired, foggy, or have a headache, **sometimes all you need is water** (or a break from reading this book, haha!).

Some of your most important post-op instructions will include keeping track of your fluid and protein intake. Developing the habit of drinking at least **sixty-four ounces of water** per day and eating a minimum of sixty grams of protein per day before surgery will make tracking after surgery so much easier.

Small children need slightly less water than adults and adolescents, which is why this guideline is not highlighted as family-friendly.

I recommend you buy yourself a cool, new water bottle. I love the ones with a loop at the top, so I can hook it around my finger when I have my hands full.

Take your water bottle everywhere for a visual reminder to drink water often. Soon, it will become as important to you as having your car keys when you head out the door.

After surgery, it can be difficult to drink enough. You will start with very small sips. After you are home from the hospital and start trying more foods, you will likely be advised to stop drinking thirty minutes before and after meals to allow room for food in your stomach without enlarging it and to prevent dumping syndrome.[28] I recommend that patients start practicing not drinking with meals before surgery. Many patients have expressed that it is one of the hardest behaviors to adopt after surgery.

Staying hydrated after surgery is very important. Dehydration can lead to nausea and vomiting, lightheadedness, and fainting. If you are struggling to stay hydrated, please contact your surgeon.

With that in mind, I have heard about patients going to IV bars for fluid and vitamin infusions after bariatric surgery. YIKES! Please keep your medical care with your medical team, which knows your history and specific needs. It's easy for your surgeon to order an outpatient IV infusion if needed. A doctor should determine decisions such as those.

BODY MASS INDEX (BMI)

Your physicians and bariatric team monitor your BMI as you work on weight loss and improved health. Some tracking apps also show your BMI, which is calculated based on the height and weight you provide.

Remember, the goal is to achieve and maintain a **BMI below 30**, out of the obesity range. I have found that a BMI of 27 tends to be where many patients maintain their weight loss. This is still in the overweight category—however, it is out of the red zone because it is no longer in the obese classification.

Many patients do achieve a BMI under 25 in the healthy range. Still, your BMI is not the ultimate determinant of your success. You should look at overall health and quality of life—especially mature women who need to maintain bone density. Again, your primary care provider and specialists will help you make these considerations.

BODY FAT PERCENTAGE

An easy way to measure your body fat percentage is with a digital bathroom scale with bioelectrical impedance analysis (BIA) capability. You can purchase this type of scale in warehouse stores, like Walmart or Costco, or online. Just look to see if the scale you are purchasing measures body fat percentage.

Foot-to-foot BIA on a bathroom scale uses a very light electrical current (you can't feel it). The current goes in one foot, takes the path of least resistance up your leg and down the other, then out that foot. The electrical current travels more quickly through water-based or lean mass than fat mass, so you receive a value based on that ratio. Accuracy can vary, but ensuring you are hydrated every time you measure will improve accuracy.[29] The trend you observe over days and weeks will be most helpful.

Tracking your body fat percentage can confirm you are losing primarily fat and not excess lean mass (muscle, water, bone density). Maintain as much lean mass as possible after surgery for strength, a healthy metabolism, and overall health and functionality. You can do this by ensuring you eat enough protein and using your muscles for planned strengthening activities at least twice weekly. Use it or lose it, right?

I do not recommend setting a goal related to your body fat percentage unless you are an athlete or a physician has recommended it. Instead, simply use this measurement to ensure you are losing primarily fat.

If you are losing weight, but your body fat percentage is staying the same or increasing, you are losing more lean mass (water, muscle, possibly bone density). If you see this as a trend and you are not dehydrated, reach out to your bariatric team.

BODY CIRCUMFERENCES

I remember telling Kelsey she had lost seventeen inches (the most I had seen yet) off of her abdomen or waist circumference. I held up my measuring tape and showed her the preoperative size, making a circle with the tape. Then, I placed it around her waist, comparing it to her current size. We both had tears in our eyes. It was hard to remember the previous version of her. She actually agreed to be our poster girl and had a billboard of her standing in one pant leg of her old jeans. She was half the size!

Likewise, Al Roker from the *Today* show (one of the most loveable people on TV, in my opinion) posted a photo on Instagram. In it, he held up a pair of jeans that looked like he could fit two of himself in them.

The post stated:

> *Hard to believe it was 20 years ago today, I wore these jeans to my #gastricbypass at 340 lbs and here I am today. It's still a struggle but I'm never going back. I may have setbacks but I work on it every day.*

Like Kelsey, Mr. Roker has also been through a lot. He spoke openly about a major extended health scare and hospitalization due to pulmonary embolism (blood clots in the lungs) in late 2022. But clearly, he never gives up.

If you don't have a place to put your measurements in your tracking app, please keep them on paper. I encourage you to measure your neck, upper arm, lower arm, chest, abdomen, hips, thigh, and calf. The measurements are helpful in understanding how your body is changing after surgery. Sometimes, patients aren't losing pounds, but they are losing inches. This is usually due to water retention. **The number on the scale does not always provide an accurate representation of what is happening**.

For most of these measurements, simply use a soft measuring tape around the middle portion of each body part. For your chest, you can go across the nipple line or directly under the bra line. For your abdominal or waist measurement, use your belly button or navel and measure in line with it for consistent tracking since your waist or the smallest part of your belly will move down as you lose weight. For your hips, slide the measuring tape up and down to find the widest part of your hips. When measuring your thigh, find the top of your kneecap. Then, measure how many inches above that you will place the measuring tape.

It is helpful if someone else does your measurements and uses the same technique every time for consistency. Take measurements at least once per month. You will appreciate them even more if you hit a plateau or stall in weight loss pounds but find that you are still losing inches.

WEIGHT

When it comes to your weight, you can weigh yourself once or twice per week to determine which direction you are moving in. Weighing more often will show small fluctuations that don't give a good indication of the overall trend.

Weigh yourself first thing in the morning with no clothes on or in your underwear, after you go to the bathroom, and before you eat or drink for consistency.

If you don't want to track your weight, that is no problem. Use your circumferences, photos, and how your clothes fit. Focus on the non-scale victories (NSVs) regarding your health and quality of life!

PHOTOS

Don't wait to take a "before picture." You'll probably lose two pounds by the time you finish this book simply because you are paying more attention to everything. Your transformation starts now!

Everyone hates getting their before photo taken, well, almost everyone. But I have never had someone regret taking a before picture when it is put side by side with an after picture or two. Many patients become emotional. What could be better positive reinforcement that all your hard work is paying off than seeing the physical difference after the changes you have undergone?

Many bariatric programs will take a photo for you. If they don't offer, feel free to ask. You can also take photos at home. It can be nice to have a private version of your before and after photos in a swimsuit, workout clothes, or even your underwear. This way, you can better compare how your body is changing.

Some hospitals will ask you if they can use your photos for marketing, but you are not obligated to do so. And they cannot use them without your written consent, so don't worry. Your photos are a part of your protected health information under HIPAA, just like the rest of your medical record.

It can also be fun to share your photos with support group members. Deb enjoys new patients' disbelief when the current 145-pound version of herself shows a pre-op patient the 330-pound version of herself. You would never imagine that they are the same person.

VITAMINS

Another habit to develop before surgery is to

take a multivitamin. A multivitamin will help provide nutritional support for optimal health before and after surgery. I usually tell patients, "You get what you pay for," when they ask me which brands are best. Some surgeons will tell you the best multivitamin is "the one you will take." Please get *your* surgeon's recommendation.

Your bariatric team will advise you on **your specific vitamin regimen**. Please don't take this into your own hands. Too much of the wrong supplements can cause serious side effects.

Additionally, nutritional supplements are not regulated by the FDA like medications are. You can look for the "USP" symbol on the bottle, which tells you your supplement has been third-party tested for purity and potency, or check the manufacturer's website to determine if they have completed their own testing from an outside lab. Consumerlab.com is a great website for information on nutritional products.

And finally, don't forget to follow up long term with your primary care provider on your vitamin and mineral levels. Insurance will only cover some tests for a certain period after surgery. So, levels like your vitamin D, thyroid function, and iron will need to be managed by your PCP, as these tend to be chronic problems. You can ask for your surgeon's guidelines so you know how to plan.

ACTIVITY

START NOW, HERE'S HOW

You knew it was coming, even though you've probably heard it before—staying active does not have to mean working out at the gym, lifting weights, going to exercise classes, or getting on a treadmill. There are so many choices, and you can create your own bank of options for staying active.

I do love going to the gym, but I don't do it all that often. I spend most of my active time walking and playing with the kids, hiking, swimming, doing family bedtime yoga, cleaning the house, working in the yard, or having a "dance party" in the kitchen with my girls.

You don't have to look at activity as a "workout" or "exercise." Do the things you love, but for balanced health, strength, and functionality, make a conscious effort to complete

strengthening, cardiovascular, and stretching activities regularly.

Remember to talk to your doctor before starting a new routine. As a guideline, strengthening activities should be completed *at least* twice per week and involves force or resistance against your muscles, like weights, calisthenics (using your own body weight), and Pilates. Yoga is also great because you can accomplish strengthening and stretching at the same time.

Cardiovascular exercises, such as walking, biking, elliptical, swimming, and hiking, can be done daily. Work your way up to at least thirty minutes four times weekly if you can. Always start with the amount you can tolerate and gradually increase your activity level.

Stretching is more effective after our muscles are warm. Complete a warm-up of five to ten minutes to get the blood flowing to all major muscle groups, then do some stretching to help prevent strains, stiffness, and injuries. Stretching also helps with our daily functionality through increased flexibility, range of motion, and better posture.

Again, you don't have to go to the gym to achieve an active lifestyle. There is so much we can do right at home with our own body weight, and everything counts! I even do push-ups on the edge of the stove while making dinner as my kids yell, "Mom, don't get burned!" For more (safer) ideas, take a look at *Your Anytime, Anywhere Guide to Being Active* in the resources section.

The current Physical Activity Guidelines for Americans is to complete a minimum of 150 minutes of moderate activity per week.[30] Moderate activity refers to movement that elevates our heart rate into a moderate intensity zone, approximately sixty-five to seventy-five percent of our maximum heart rate, which is 220 minus your age.

My favorite way to track this is with my smartwatch because it shows me how many more "zone" minutes I need. It counts every minute that I am active with my heart rate up, whether carrying in the groceries, walking the dog, or sweating at the gym. The app or website you choose for tracking will help you set goals for activity.

Don't feel like you need to get hung up on the details—just start moving more. You can do that. Get up out of your seat, walk, create a short morning routine, and have fun doing whatever works for you. Remember, we are working to develop **lifelong, healthy habits**, not temporary torture.

As previously discussed, regular physical activity can **prevent disease, improve physical and mental function, and boost your energy and mood**. But don't forget about endorphins. Endorphins are hormones released when we stress our bodies during activities such as brisk walking, swimming, hiking, and dancing. Endorphins attach to opioid receptors in the brain's reward centers. This means that **endorphins are a natural painkiller**.[31] Movement really is medicine for the mind and body.

So who's up for some mood and energy-boosting, pain-killing activity? Great, make a plan! Look at your calendar and schedule planned physical activity as often as you can. Even better, make it part of your regular routines. Take a daily walk and **get your heart rate up** doing it! There will always be good weeks and bad weeks when it comes to your routines—that is normal! Just keep going.

STRESS, SLEEP & MINDFULNESS

Remember to check your tracking website or app for sleep, stress, and mindfulness monitoring options if you would like. Adequate rest and reflecting on how we're feeling emotionally are important aspects of our mental health and well-being.

Physical and emotional stress are associated with higher levels of the hormone cortisol in our bodies. These higher levels of cortisol can lead to weight gain through mechanisms like increased appetite and cravings for high-fat, high-sugar foods.[32] Managing our stress is essential to achieving and maintaining weight loss.

That being said, there are a few things I feel we don't talk about enough regarding our health. They tie directly to our emotional and physical health. These things are sunlight, fresh air, and our breathing. Taking time to

go outside for a dose of sunlight, fresh air, and some deep breathing can make a positive difference in your day. They are an essential part of a healthy lifestyle and good mental health.

Additionally, we've all heard how important it is to

get enough sleep. But did you know that poor sleep can be hard on your heart and contribute to weight gain? Poor sleep is even more dangerous if you suffer from sleep apnea. If you snore, wake up gasping, or suffer from severe daytime sleepiness, it may be time for a sleep study—please talk to your doctor. For now, try to create healthier sleep habits by getting to bed earlier, avoiding screen time two hours before bed, and limiting caffeine use. And, of course, regular physical activity will also contribute to quality sleep!

In our home, we love the calming and relaxing effects of guided meditations that start with some slow, deep breaths. There are many meditation apps, websites, and YouTube videos, most of which are free. You can find meditations for two minutes to thirty minutes or more. I enjoy

guided meditation practices for sleep, focus, stress relief, anxiety, and mindfulness. My favorite app is the Australian-based Smiling Mind. These are simple and fun guided meditations for the whole family. And who doesn't want a lovely Australian accent guiding them to sleep? You can even choose a male or female voice.

LET'S GO!

I'm not sure if it's good or bad that I just crammed weeks of weight loss counseling into one chapter—I'll let you be the judge. I hope you gained some new information to use as you actively create your new story, the best version of yourself. If you are feeling overwhelmed, we will simplify things in the next chapter by creating some actionable steps.

Although, there is no time like the present! How about a walk? Yes, right now (if it's not too late at night). Close the book, put on your athletic shoes, grab your sunglasses or jacket, and head outside. I'm going too—enjoy!

Chapter 11

Making It Last

Water? I drink plenty of water; I drink whiskey and water.
— Non-surgical Patient

I cannot make this stuff up. That was a direct quote from a lovely man who spent long hours at the office. He struggled to invest time and energy into meal planning and prep because he lived alone. Everyone is starting at such a different point with eating and exercise habits. There is no one-size-fits-all program. You need to **start where you are ready** to begin making changes, whether that is drinking water without whiskey or starting a daily walking routine.

Have you downloaded a tracking app? Why not? If you and technology don't get along, use paper. You can find downloadable and printable tracking pages online or make your own. Your bariatric surgeon and team will appreciate that you are already tracking your water, protein, and activity specifically.

GOALS AND ACCOUNTABILITY

As you set goals, one of the best things you can do is **stay flexible**—please don't place unrealistic timelines on yourself. You should plan on achieving a realistic weight loss goal after surgery, but you won't have exact control over *when* that happens. Every BODY is different. You *can* control how well you follow the guidelines your surgeon has given you for success.

Staying accountable by attending support groups and encouraging loved ones to practice healthy habits along with you is another proven predictor of success. Remember to keep your associations with other patients positive. Especially online, lean toward the ones making progress in their transformations, not those struggling or looking for ways to "cheat." Keeping regular post-op appointments with your bariatric team and primary care provider is the best way to hold yourself accountable and ensure you are on track.

START SMALL

Starting small is a great way to help you build momentum. Identify your priorities, be specific, and choose **one change** to fully commit to so you don't get overwhelmed. Just get used to tracking things before changing your entire diet. As you become more mindful, you will identify areas where you are ready to improve.

Some of the simplest and most crucial changes to start working on, in addition to tracking, are eating more slowly, chewing well, eating from smaller plates, and taking smaller bites. You will be surprised how hard this is, but it is critical. I will explain why in the next chapter.

Gordon B. Hinckley, one of my favorite authors, was known for using the analogy of a gate. He shared,

> "Have you ever looked at a great farm gate that opens and closes? If you look at the hinge, it moves ever so little. Just a little movement of that hinge creates tremendous consequences out of the perimeter. That is the way it is with our lives. It is the little decisions that make the great differences in our lives."[33]

Whether you decide to have surgery or not, there are small decisions you can make starting today to impact your health and well-being positively in the long run. It is the sum of all our small **decisions**, as well as the big ones, that **mean everything** when it comes to our circumstances in life.

MAKE A PLAN!

As Tony Robbins proclaims in his Breakthrough app, **"Turn your shoulds into musts!"** He states:

> *Everybody's got a list of shoulds... I should work out; I should spend more time with my kids; I should make more calls... And you do it some of the time, but not all of the time, because if it's really uncomfortable, you don't do all of your shoulds. And when you don't do them, what happens? You beat yourself up; you should all over yourself, don't you? You should all over yourself. That does not make it better; it lowers your energy, and then it becomes a cycle. So, what we need to do is figure out where our standard is and raise it. Because if you look at anyone who has something they want or anything in your life that you're proud of, it's because you have a higher standard than most people in that area." So, how do we raise the standard? We need a plan!*[34]

In the resources section, I have *Your Bombshell Action Plan* ready for you. By the time you finish reading this book, you will have increased understanding and should feel empowered to act upon this knowledge. Or fill it out now if you are ready!

Here's my suggestion: stand up, take a deep breath, reach your hands to the sky, then exhale as you lower your arms. Now get excited! I like to bounce around and throw a few air punches. I know I'm weird. Move around, put on your favorite song, and dance! Let out a wooohooo!! Whatever works for you! But once you are in that higher energy state, you are ready to make your plan!

REPETITION

Think about learning to drive or ride a bicycle. It was so scary and overwhelming at first. But you did a little bit at a time. You had a lot of help and support. Sometimes, you fell, but it got easier along the way. The more you practice and expose yourself to the information you want to implement, the more familiar and automatic these concepts will become.

You have to keep doing it over and over and over. Even patients years out from surgery can fall back into old habits and get sidetracked from bariatric behaviors. Please don't look at any of these changes as a temporary means to an end. The habits you are practicing now are **lifelong** for **long-term success**.

DINING OUT

Another easy change to start implementing is to

dine out less. Eating outside of the home is directly correlated to weight gain.[35] This includes sit-down restaurants, fast food, convenience items, and cafeterias. You might be surprised at how often you eat out per week if you add it up. Include sugary drinks, which usually have as many calories as a small meal.

To stay mindful, I add a little red bowl icon to my calendar when I eat out. Any time you don't prepare your food, there are guaranteed hidden calories, excess fats, sugars, cholesterol, additives, salt (sodium), and other things you don't want more of in your diet. I'm not saying that you shouldn't eat out, but there is a health-conscious way to do it, and *minimizing* how often you dine out will most certainly impact your success.

Here are some pointers for dining out: To keep large portions from undoing all your hard work, ask for a takeout container when you order your meal or split an entree with someone else. Having half as much food in front of you as you eat is a great way to avoid overeating.

Don't forget to ask for dressings and sauces on the side. Try dipping your fork in the sauce or dressing, then stabbing your food rather than pouring condiments. Avoid fried foods and skip the potatoes, which will likely give you excess starch (carbohydrates). Baked sweet potatoes or yams are better if you do decide to have a potato, but watch the butter and skip the brown sugar.

Also, skip the extra carbs at the beginning of the meal, whether it's bread or chips and salsa. Lastly, if you want to indulge and split a dessert with someone, skip the carbs (bread, potatoes, rice, pasta, etc.) with your dinner to help balance it out.

What's more, it will come as no surprise that I've yet to meet anyone who can eat a pasta dinner at a restaurant without stalling their weight loss. Save the pasta for special occasions. I have found it interesting that some patients no longer crave or enjoy pasta after bariatric surgery, so that can be a bonus if pasta is currently one of your weaknesses.

One of my favorite sayings attributed to motivational speaker Zig Ziglar is, "Don't trade what you want for what you want right now." You don't need to deprive yourself entirely. Still, I challenge you to **find a balance between self-discipline and enjoying life** when it comes to dining out. That balance will allow you to maintain weight loss and better health.

SELF-CARE

Don't forget always to come back to your why. When you want to eat the next slice of pizza or piece of candy, you've got to remember why you ultimately chose to start doing things differently. And remember, the more you exercise your muscles of self-discipline and experience the benefits, the easier it will get.

Focus on what you get more of rather than what you're cutting out because it does not serve the person you are becoming. Eat more healthy lean protein, water, fruits, colorful vegetables, and whole grains instead of processed grains. Focus on taking more evening walks, enjoying more active fun, spending more time on mindfulness, and caring more for yourself.

The My Fitness Pal app tells me, "Sweating is self-care," under the section with pre-made workouts. I can't say that statement makes me want to drop what I'm doing, put on some exercise clothes, and do the Full Body Burn workout, but I like the mindset shift that it creates.

We do so much for other people, often at the expense of our own well-being. Give yourself permission to care for yourself and practice healthy habits. Doing so can help you show up as your best, healthiest, happiest self!

MAINTAIN A HEALTHY METABOLISM

In biology, change refers to how organisms adapt and evolve. Our bodies are designed to survive. While the world has changed drastically over the last few thousand years, our bodies are still programmed to prevent starvation. We have yet to evolve to the easy access, high-calorie food that surrounds most of us—but unfortunately, not all of us.

As under-evolved organisms in this sense, our metabolism, or how much energy our body uses, slows down when we don't eat for long periods. As a result, the body can survive longer. However, with a slowed metabolism, our body won't utilize as many calories and consumed excess calories will be converted to stored energy or fat. We call this the starvation and storage process.

The commonly referred to "yo-yo effect" is another process leading to weight regain from a slowed metabolism. This time, a slowed metabolism occurs due to muscle loss from extended calorie restriction. Just as with skipping meals, over-restricting your daily calorie intake over time can cause your body to utilize fewer calories.

So, how can we combat these processes and keep a healthy metabolism? First, do not go for long periods without eating during the day—ideally, three to four hours should be the maximum. It is especially important after surgery because you can only eat a little at a time. You have to eat often enough to achieve your nutrition goals. You don't need to wake up at night to eat, but your last, small, protein-based snack about three hours after dinner often achieves your daily protein goal.

Secondly, keep your muscles healthy. I don't mean you need to hire Beau at the gym and pay him lots of money to count to ten while you almost give yourself a hernia lifting weights. I just mean use it or lose it. Muscle is your most metabolically active tissue. So **healthy muscles help you burn more calories, lose weight faster, and make you less likely to regain weight**.[36] Break the regain cycles—don't skip meals, and keep those muscles healthy! Remember to see the resources section for ideas on how to do so!

PATIENCE AND CONSISTENCY

Please give yourself some grace. This is the rest of your life, remember. It took time to gain weight, and it will take time to lose it. Our bodies sometimes even combat the weight loss process, as you may have experienced.

You know what you need to do. Consistency is the bridge that connects your dreams to reality. Regarding your health, every small step you take toward your goals matters. Whether eating nutritious meals, being active, or getting enough sleep, each action contributes to a healthier and happier you.

Remember, it's not about being perfect but showing up for yourself every day. Embrace the power of small, consistent actions, and watch as they transform into lasting habits. Celebrate your progress along the way, and know that **every choice you make in favor of your health is an investment in your future well-being**.

So, stay committed, stay focused, and keep pushing forward. You've got this! The next chapter will highlight crucial guidelines to keep you healthy and feeling well after surgery.

Chapter 12

Guidelines that Seem Simple yet Are Incredibly Important

The little things aren't little—they're everything.
— Tony Robbins

We've covered a lot of ground. Still, we need to discuss further some behaviors you will be working on. These behaviors may seem like no-brainers, but they are vitally important to your well-being after surgery.

EAT SLOWLY AND CHEW WELL

Let's slow down. After surgery, your stomach and gastrointestinal tract are healing. There is swelling and inflammation resulting from an invasive procedure. Even months and years later, your smaller stomach needs a slow approach. Taking small bites, chewing each bite twenty to thirty times, and waiting between bites is a practice that will make or break your recovery and long-term results. Give your stomach small amounts at a time to minimize its workload breaking down food. Chewing your food well also minimizes this work. Waiting in between bites gives your stomach time to register the food and send signals to your brain about how full and how much distress (if any) it is in.

You may experience food intolerances as your stomach is healing. Food intolerances are especially common when advancing to the next diet stage. Specifically, you will progress from liquid to puree and then to solid textures. **Take small bites <u>slowly</u>** to learn whether or not your stomach is ready for certain foods before introducing too much.

You will also quickly learn to avoid one last bite too many. Many people have strange signs of fullness, such as burping, tightness, or a lump in their throat. If you aren't sure if you should take one last bite, don't. It may lead to stomach upset in many forms, including regurgitation or vomiting.

In addition to eating from smaller plates, many patients use smaller forks and spoons, even baby utensils, to help them slowly eat small bites. Seeing a full, small plate become empty can help provide a visual cue that you are finished. A full, small plate sounds more satisfying than a partially empty, large plate, right? Also, find ways to distract yourself between bites. You can use conversation, read, or play a game on your phone for ideas.

A good guideline to start practicing with is ten minutes per ounce. Try it. You will be amazed how little food it is, so the smaller bites, chewing well, and waiting in between will help. I know you won't have thirty minutes to sit and eat every time after surgery (once you have progressed to roughly three-ounce meals), so get creative. Start with one bite and complete a task between bites, but be sure you do not fall into the habit of grazing or mindless eating.

Shakes and smoothies are a lifesaver when you don't have much time because you can slowly sip while doing other things. However, your body will always utilize and get the most out of real food, so try not to become too dependent on supplemental protein from powders, shakes, and bars. You will want to have them for when you can't get to real food, but try to save them for when you really need them.

STAY HYDRATED, BUT DON'T DRINK WITH MEALS

Staying hydrated after surgery is key to preventing problems and feeling well. Although, you will likely be advised to avoid drinking fluid thirty minutes before and thirty minutes after meals. Remember, you don't want to overexpand a healing stomach with water *and* food.

Sip regularly throughout the day, stopping before and after meals, to ensure you achieve your hydration goal. It is one thing to take a small sip of water to help your food go down, but please don't sip regularly while eating. Filling up too fast can also lead to grazing throughout the day rather than mindful eating because you will want to eat again so soon.

Don't sell yourself short by bending your guidelines. The research has been done to provide you with the best path, so follow it! Again, start practicing this habit now, as many bariatric patients say that not drinking with meals and not being able to chug large amounts of water was one of the hardest adjustments they had to make after surgery.

PROTEIN FIRST

Eating your protein first is another essential guideline. You will recall that protein intake is the primary means for tracking your nourishment after surgery. Achieving your recommended protein intake (and taking your supplements) reduces your risk for nutrition problems.

As you track your protein intake and choose more protein sources, you will learn what sixty to one hundred grams of protein look like. You shouldn't have a hard time eating this much protein before surgery, but you may for a while after surgery. **Protein-based foods will fill you up faster**.

After advancing back to a regular diet, some patients report being tempted not to eat protein first because they want to eat more food. Doing so can lead you to eat excess carbs and snack foods and not achieve your protein goal. And while noticing you can eat potato chip after potato chip may take you back to "the good ole days," remember **why** you don't want to go back.

When you make your plate, give yourself roughly three ounces of **protein** (or half your plate). Then add some **nutritious low-carb veggies**, a little **healthy fat**, and a **carbohydrate** (see the resources section): starchy veggies like corn, potato, or sweet potato, sweet squashes, peas—which are a legume—OR pasta, bread, rice, quinoa or other grains, beans, lentils, or fruit. Eat the protein first, remember to chew well and eat slowly, then eat whatever you have room left for regarding the rest.

For good nutrition, it is vital to have a variety of fruits, vegetables, legumes, nuts, seeds, healthy fats, and whole grains in our diet. So, choose high-quality, unprocessed items that will give you the most nutrition for a small amount. Farther out from surgery, it will get easier to eat more, in addition to your protein. But please don't feel like you need to force anything. Talk to your dietician if you struggle to eat a balanced diet after advancing to a regular diet postoperatively.

EAT SMALL, FREQUENT MEALS

If you have been logging your food, you will be familiar with this concept. There are multiple benefits when it comes to eating small, frequent meals.

First, your body receives **regular nourishment for sustained energy**. Secondly, small meals (roughly the size of your fist) ensure that you are much **less likely to consume excess calories,** which if not utilized, may be stored as fat. Lastly, after surgery, when you can not eat more than a few bites at a time, it is vital that you eat *often* enough to **achieve healthy nutrient levels and meet your protein goal** of sixty to one hundred grams per day.

WALK & MOVE YOUR BODY

This may seem obvious, but there are so many reasons why walking is critical. It will help prevent postoperative complications like blood clots, respiratory depression, pneumonia, and constipation. It can help with pain management and healing. And it is crucial to achieve your goals for improved health.

Please recall, as you lose weight rapidly, it is essential to use your muscles so they don't atrophy (waste away). You need them to maintain functionality and strength. Further, **maintaining your muscle mass will contribute to a healthy metabolism, making it easier to lose weight and keep it off**.

Walking will help you develop and maintain good cardiorespiratory health or a healthy heart and lungs. And exercise releases endorphins, which help us feel good, leading to better mental health and quality of life. Living an active lifestyle can also help prevent disease (including certain types of cancer), increase insulin sensitivity (which can prevent diabetes), improve blood flow and circulation, and help our bodies eliminate toxins. It also provides benefits regarding mental clarity, depression, anxiety, and sleep quality.[37]

While it is important to have a balanced exercise routine, including strengthening, flexibility, and cardiovascular exercise, walking is something most of us do every day. It takes minimal effort to increase the amount of walking that we do, leading to those incredible benefits.

It may seem simple, but adding more walking, especially brisk walking for thirty minutes or more, will make all the difference. Anyone can work their way up to this. Yes, even those of you who use a walker or a wheelchair. Have your doctor order some physical therapy in the pool (hydrotherapy) and start your walking there. You will be amazed at the mental, emotional, and physical benefits of moving your body more. Every bit makes a difference!

TAKE MEDICATIONS AND SUPPLEMENTS AS DIRECTED

Everything your surgeon and bariatric team recommends is based on decades of scientific research to provide the best patient outcomes. Your surgeon thoughtfully prescribes each medication and supplement with a purpose for you.

Please **follow instructions closely, ask questions, and have everything on hand before surgery**. The one exception may be your prescription pain medication, which often is not prescribed until you are discharged from the hospital because it is a controlled substance.

There may be some things you end up not needing, like over-the-counter Gas-X or even the stronger or opioid pain medication, but make sure you have them anyway. You will be so grateful when and if you do need them.

Review each medication's purpose and instructions for use. Know what your dose is and how often you need to take it. Does it need to be taken with food? Do you need to ensure that it is not taken with other medications or supplements due to interactions? These are vital considerations that you don't want to try and figure out when you are tired and in pain. Be sure you are clear beforehand. Creating a schedule on your phone or on paper can be very helpful.

Especially for sleeve patients, if you are prescribed omeprazole or another type of antacid, please take it as directed. Managing postoperative acid reflux is very important in the prevention of ulcers. Imagine your poor stomach trying to heal after surgery and dealing with excess acid, which damages those sensitive tissues.

Excess acid may be a long-term condition after surgery. Still, it can be managed as you follow your bariatric guidelines and take your antacid. Eat slowly, chew well, keep your portions small, don't eat late at night (which contributes to acid reflux), and don't lie down for at least two hours after eating. Lastly, if you were not prescribed an antacid and you start having any symptoms of acid reflux, especially abdominal pain, please contact your surgeon as soon as possible for evaluation and treatment. If you have not had surgery yet and you have untreated GERD or acid reflux, be sure to make your surgeon aware. There could be an underlying cause, such as a hiatal hernia or an H. pylori infection, that needs addressing.

I hope the guidelines and techniques I have provided in the preceding chapters will help ensure your journey is as smooth and successful as possible. Remember that everyone on your bariatric team is on your side, even though sometimes it will feel like you are given unnecessary tasks or challenges. It is all to increase your safety and likelihood of long-term success. This is surgery that has lifelong effects. It's kind of a big deal, right? Take your time to learn, grow, and change. Do it right for yourself.

Next, we will cover some topics that bariatric patients feel are most important for you to be aware of before surgery.

Chapter 13

Wisdom from Bariatric Patients

Don't judge me by my success. Judge me by how many times I fall and get back up again.
— Nelson Mandela

Nurses are superstitious. Full moon: It will be a crazy night at the hospital. Say "quiet" or "slow" at work: Everyone hates you now because the opposite will come true. Seriously, these are REAL phenomena. That's why it's fitting that this is Chapter 13. Some of what you read might scare you. I share it because you should know the possibilities. Not everything you read from these patients will happen along your journey, but won't it be nice to be prepared when *some* do?

It's also important to note that some of these answers pertain to the challenges patients face socially after surgery. As I've expressed, I hope we can continue to broaden our perspectives to be less judgmental and more helpful to bariatric patients in personal and social environments.

The following headings are quotes from patients' responses when I asked them what they thought was most important for others to know regarding weight loss surgery. This chapter is not a comprehensive list of pros and cons but some things you might not hear about before surgery. It may feel like there are a lot of negatives, but I've included them to be helpful. **The more you know about**

challenges others have faced, the better equipped you will be, allowing you to focus on recovery and better health.

SURGERY IS JUST ONE TOOL

I know you get it by now. However, this is an important lesson for bariatric patients to take away from surgery long term. As dedicated as you may be, life will find ways to wriggle in and make it hard for you to stay on track. Holidays, stress, loneliness, boredom, going out, and family get-togethers are common obstacles that can lead to derailment. Those things aren't going to go away. The goal is for you to learn how to navigate these times and **utilize all of your tools for lifelong healthy habits**.

In addition to weight loss surgery, your tools consist of self-monitoring and planning ahead, goals and accountability, increased activity, better food choices, and following up with your health care providers. Remember, this is a team approach, and you have an entire crew to support you in your hard work.

SOME PEOPLE HAVE A HARDER TIME WITH WHAT THEIR BODY LOOKS LIKE AFTER SURGERY THAN BEFORE

This is another difficult topic. I think a lot of patients suffer in silence when it comes to their post-surgery bodies. We all have things that we don't like about our bodies. I have terribly wide feet, and when I was a teenager, my physical therapist said, "I bet you don't fall through the ice with those!" Then he waddled around like a duck, quacked, and laughed. What a lovely thing to say to an insecure and impressionable teenager.

When it comes to weight loss surgery, you may be trading some of your current insecurities for new ones. After one hundred or two hundred pounds of weight loss, you may look thin, healthy, and normal on the outside but have layers of loose skin that you have carefully tucked with the right clothing. No one knows but you and perhaps an intimate partner, as you look in the mirror, witnessing your changing body.

If you're wondering how significant others respond to how the body changes after surgery, many patients report increased activity in the bedroom. One woman, who is mature in years, even expressed being slightly overwhelmed at her husband's increased interest. However, I don't think she was complaining.

Despite this trade-off of loose skin and the challenge of coming to terms with your new body image, I can't recall one patient who wished they didn't have surgery because of the way their body looks. It will take time for you to adjust physically and mentally. Be patient with yourself. Talk to others and get help. And remember, the reason you chose weight loss surgery was not to have a perfect body. It was for your improved health and quality of life.

I WAS SURPRISED HOW SOON I STARTED TO HAVE A LOT MORE ENERGY

Do you remember the thrill of being young and having so much energy that you didn't know what to do with it? Some patients report having this kind of energy again after surgery. It doesn't happen for everyone and has much to do with how well you meet your nutrition goals. Yet, most patients at least talk about how **breathing and getting around are easier**.

The lovely lady who made this statement works on farmland with her husband. Before surgery, she talked about struggling to breathe as she walked out into the pastures. I remember how excited she was to tell me she felt like she flew across the fields to meet her husband one day. She was also completing projects she never thought she would find the energy for.

Another patient started painting and remodeling her home. Yet another started traveling again. It's amazing how we take these abilities for granted: being able to climb a flight of stairs, carry in the groceries, keep up with the kids or grandkids, and travel. Only those who have lost these abilities truly understand and fully appreciate the gifts they are.

IT'S PHYSICALLY AND MENTALLY TAXING, MORE THAN ANYONE TELLS YOU

I know this is the opposite of what I just told you, but every patient's experience is different. Surgery is a big deal. The more you can learn and prepare for life after surgery, the better—you need the time after surgery to focus on a healthy recovery, follow diet stages, and keep up with medication regimens. It is not the time to learn on the fly.

Even patients with many months or years of preparation may have something unexpected to deal with after surgery. Prepare physically and mentally by reading, talking to your providers and other patients, and practicing bariatric habits. Your groundwork will arm you with the ability to navigate the parts outside your control.

I use what I call the bariatric spectrum of post-op possibilities. On the one end is the patient with a completely smooth recovery, minimal pain, easy diet transitions, and no complications. On the other end of the spectrum is the patient who struggles with keeping pain managed, experiences almost every post-op nuisance (nausea, difficulty swallowing, constipation, gas, etc.), suffers discomfort with diet transitions, and possibly deals with complications.

Smooth Recovery - - - - - - - - - - - - - - Difficult Recovery

There is no way to know how your body will tolerate bariatric surgery. Preparing for the worst and hoping for the best is always a good idea!

BE CAREFUL WITH SUGAR

This response is from one of my favorite patients who has worked so hard to transform her life. After two years of weight loss surgery success, she found herself rationalizing regular trips to Starbucks for specialty coffee drinks because "At least I wasn't having a cigarette." Unfortunately, the high-calorie, high-sugar beverages led to some weight regain. She talked about how she got rid of her bigger clothes, and now her current clothes are tight. Her frustration and disappointment were visible.

These types of setbacks are not uncommon. I hope she will view this experience as an opportunity for growth and resolve to replace her trips to Starbucks with some fun little outing or distraction. It's funny how we can find ourselves so innocently in these types of situations. Regular trips to Starbucks are normal for many people, but it is helpful to remember that we want to belong to the *minority* when it comes to weight, not the majority. Unfortunately, the majority in this country is not at a healthy weight.

By not participating in unhealthy social norms, we may slightly stand out. That's okay because it ultimately means we stand out in a good way. We are setting ourselves apart as positive role models, and there are other ways to have fun besides indulging in food and drink.

Avoid empty-calorie, sugary drinks—even fruit juices. It is always better to get your fruit in whole form.

As the mom of a beautiful young woman, I know this patient thinks about modeling healthy behavior for her daughter. I am certain that she will also consider the importance of giving herself some grace and demonstrating that it's okay to make mistakes. That is how we learn and grow. That is how we become even better.

DON'T WAIT

This response came from a lovely woman who felt an extreme sense of urgency as her health was in a sharp decline. She proudly shares that after surgery, she is off of sixteen medications and is able to be there for her family, which is so important to her, especially as a caregiver.

I cannot count how many times patients have said to me in post-op follow-up, "I wish I had done it sooner." Many of them agonized for years and decades, wondering if it was time to quit the yo-yo diet cycle and seek surgical intervention. It probably doesn't help that every few months, there is a new weight loss fad that promises to be the solution to your struggles. Usually, if it sounds too good to be true, it is.

Despite wishing they had surgery sooner, these patients tend to be the ones who take life by the horns after surgery and live with a newfound passion. They literally transform before our eyes. It's like they have finally become the person they knew they could be, or they are back to being the person they love. It's really beautiful.

No one *wants* to have surgery. But when you have lost the same thirty or fifty pounds repeatedly, surgery may be the best option for improved health and quality of life. Many patients delayed surgery because they didn't want to tell friends and family they had gotten to that point.

Surgery should be the last option after all efforts have been made for successful weight loss. But remember, admitting you need help and asking for it is a sign of strength, not of weakness.

THE MENTAL PART OF IT WAS HARD FOR ME—KNOWING WHEN TO STOP EATING AND LISTENING TO MY BODY, NOT MY MIND. AND BODY DYSMORPHIA IS HARD!

Andrea, a successful weight loss patient for nearly a decade, recommends the book *Intuitive Eating* by Evelyn Tribole, MS, RD. She talks about how the book taught her to be more in tune with her body regarding hunger and fullness sensations.

Not only is it helpful to read about how to cope with bariatric surgery, but you will need someone to talk to. Patients have a support person who is there physically to help. Still, it may be another person who you turn to for mental and emotional support. They could be a friend, loved one, or mental health provider. Better yet, all three!

The mental and emotional challenge of rewiring your thoughts to tell yourself it's best to only eat a little bit at a time when we are used to eating large portions is a complex aspect of the bariatric lifestyle. Please work on this *before* surgery. I'm not saying you should start eating bariatric portions, but you should begin to eat *smaller* ones. Remember, eating from smaller plates can be one way to "trick" yourself into feeling satisfied. A small portion on a small plate feels like more food than a small portion on a large plate.

Many patients talk about "that one bite too many." Sometimes, only one more bite can be the difference between feeling fine or uncomfortable after a meal. If you aren't sure, skip it. This concept is difficult to explain, but you will certainly know when you experience it after surgery. Almost all patients do. Then you can learn what your body feels like before "that one bite too many" and know when it's time to stop eating.

The best way to prevent discomfort (some patients explain it as a knot in their throat, tightness, burping, or heaviness) is by eating slowly and chewing well. This gives your body plenty of time to determine what it can tolerate and send those signals to your brain.

Lastly, body dysmorphia is a mental health diagnosis that consists of disordered thought patterns. It occurs when someone sees and imagines themself as smaller or larger than they are. In the case of postoperative bariatric patients, it is very common for one to still think of themself as a person with obesity when, in fact, their weight is healthy.

Ten years after surgery, one patient still talks about walking up to the grocery store as a 150-pound woman after surgery and still expecting to see a 300-pound woman in her window reflection. Give yourself time to adjust and use positive self-talk to help create your new, healthier self-image.

YOUR ENTIRE LIFE CHANGES. IT'S DIFFICULT GOING TO FAMILY FUNCTIONS, EVEN JUST GOING OUT WITH FRIENDS, WHEN YOU CAN'T EAT MORE THAN A COUPLE OF TABLESPOONS. IT'S NOT THAT WE DON'T LIKE THE FOOD GRANDMA MADE—WE PHYSICALLY CAN'T EAT IT. THIS WAY OF LOSING WEIGHT HAS ITS OWN SET OF CHALLENGES, AND THEY ARE NOT FUN. BUT IT IS WORTH IT IF YOU CAN GET THROUGH THEM.

I love this statement. It refers to more than one of the social challenges patients face after bariatric surgery. Especially early on, restaurants, family gatherings, and holiday meals can be challenging. Over time, you will create your own methods for navigating social eating situations. I have included some ideas in the resources section.

Patients may only tolerate a couple of ounces of food per sitting early after surgery. Also, certain textures sit heavier in the healing stomach than others, which is normal. I hear stories from patients about restaurant servers asking why they didn't like their food or are they *sure* they don't want some water with their meal, for the twentieth time.

Family members may feel offended or worried because you "aren't eating enough." As long as you follow your guidelines and listen to your body, you ARE eating enough. As frustrating as it may be, the best thing to do in this situation may be to educate those concerned about why you aren't eating more or drinking with meals. By doing so, you may save someone else the same frustration.

In a recent support group, Lisa shared that she often explains to family members that she will eat again in about three hours so they don't need to worry.

HAIR LOSS IS STRESSFUL AND SCARY—SO IS LOOSE SKIN

Most bariatric patients experience some hair loss in the first year after surgery. For women especially, this can be their most significant concern. I even had one patient tell me that she had been putting off surgery for years because she didn't want to lose hair. Unfortunately, her health declined during that period, and she finally decided her health was more important than her hair.

There are things you can do to minimize hair loss. Be sure to meet your daily protein intake requirement. Take your vitamins. You can take biotin or a hair, skin, and nails supplement. Many patients start that before surgery.

It is important to clarify that you should not take any of these supplements in higher amounts than your surgeon and dietician recommended. A fish oil supplement can also be helpful. And some patients swear by collagen peptides. For a topical approach, research different shampoos and tonics. Ask around in your groups to find out what has worked for others.

Many patients buy beautiful wigs or extensions and use them temporarily until their hair thickens up again. That may not be the solution for you, but how you cut your hair can also change how thick it looks. Remember, there are worse things than losing your hair. Hopefully, it is temporary and a worthy trade for better health if you do.

You will also read a lot about loose skin in your research. Patients who lose more weight will likely have more loose skin. However, genes, age, height, sun exposure, smoking, and how quickly you lose weight also play a role. If you are younger, your skin is more elastic. As we age, we lose elasticity in our skin, so surgery or not, most of us end up with more wobbly bits (as the fictional heroine Bridget Jones would call them) than we would like.[38]

Some patients do end up having skin removal surgery. Unfortunately, insurance doesn't usually cover it unless the skin on your belly is causing health problems like rashes leading to skin breakdown. Other areas are usually considered cosmetic, but it's worth checking your insurance policy. Talk to your primary care provider if you are considering skin removal surgery so they can document any problems excess skin is causing you and refer you to a plastic surgeon.

Hair loss and loose skin are probably two of the biggest challenges for patients regarding their body image after surgery. Please **remember you are not alone, and reach out for support.**

Try to focus on the positive effects, like having more energy, doing things easier, getting rid of medications, and enjoying better health!

IT CAN BE HARD TO DRINK PLAIN WATER

Bariatric patients should drink at least sixty-four ounces of water daily. They also typically need to stop drinking thirty minutes before and after meals to allow room for food and proper digestion. As some patients report, that can be challenging when plain water no longer tastes good.

If I had to guess, I would say about fifteen to twenty percent of patients who come for follow-up after surgery state they can't drink plain water. I could not find any statistical data on this phenomenon. There is speculation that this "water nausea" is a result of already being dehydrated or the stomach being too full. In my experience, patients report it is the taste; for others, their stomach just doesn't tolerate it, or it feels "heavy." Most patients report improvements over time.

If you experience intolerance to plain water, get creative with sugar-free, caffeine-free additions, such as sports drinks, Crystal Light, or infusions. Experiment with different flavors and mixtures. Some people do well with fifty percent sports drink or flavor add-in and fifty percent water, which can better hydrate you. Some people like the flavor to be stronger or weaker. Water infusions are even better and can add delicious flavors without unnatural additives. Cucumber, lemon, lime, strawberry, and mint are my favorites. You can find different ways to make them online.

NOT ALL HEALTHCARE PROVIDERS WILL BE SUPPORTIVE OF YOUR DECISION TO HAVE WEIGHT LOSS SURGERY

This is really sad. Just as many in the general public lack perspective, as I once did, there are still some who are charged with our care that do not support bariatric surgery.

Unfortunately, some healthcare providers have seen patients suffer from problems after weight loss surgery and have formed negative opinions because of it. Think about it—an emergency room (ER) doctor is going to hear a lot more about dehydration or nausea and vomiting after weight loss surgery than they will about a patient losing 150 lbs, getting off of ten different medications, and being able to ride their motorcycle again. Those aren't the types of things you talk about in the ER.

Not to say that problems don't occur—of course they do. But there will always be those who, no matter what the statistics show, choose to disagree. Conversely, I have seen primary care providers who opposed weight loss surgery change their minds. This occurred after observing several of their patients transform into healthier, happier individuals after weight loss surgery.

You can request a different provider who will better understand your needs if you aren't getting the care you deserve from a healthcare provider due to obvious prejudice against bariatric surgery. You have the right to unbiased care, and if you receive anything less, I encourage you to bring it to the attention of your hospital or clinic administration.

I assure you that the administrative team's goal is for you to feel comfortable and cared for. Please make them aware of shortcomings. Staff education should happen regularly; maybe it is time for another bariatric training. Please never tolerate rude or dismissive treatment.

THE BIGGEST FEAR IS REGAIN

I hear this a lot. Fear can be an effective tool when used properly. It can keep us motivated, never to go back to the way things were. Yet rather than focusing on the fear of ending up back where you started, focus on your progress and positive outcome. Follow your guidelines so you don't find yourself inching in the wrong direction, and take action if you do!

Don't put too much focus on the possibility of regaining weight. Ups and downs are normal. Have your bariatric team help you with your weight loss goal after surgery. Then, after your weight stabilizes, choose a range (I like a six to eight-pound range) for long-term maintenance. This way, the expected small fluctuations will not bother you.

My good friend, Kassi, had the gastric sleeve three years ago. She has had an incredible journey, though not without its challenges, as she works to find the balance between nutrition and a busy lifestyle. Kassi is the ultimate Bariatric

Bombshell beauty, as she proudly goes out in her cute new dresses. People swear she's aging backward. She has been open about her journey, including her struggles, but is thrilled to enjoy better health.

When Kassi started to notice weight regain, she got more serious about diet and exercise and talked to her primary care provider. She was started on weight loss medication to help get her blood sugar levels and appetite back in check. As you probably know, weight loss medications are more popular than ever. They can be another useful tool as you strive to lose weight and build better health.

However, don't get me wrong—I am not advocating weight loss medication for everyone. It has its risks, too, and more research needs to be done regarding the long-term effects. My point is to **do everything you can and talk to your doctor if you are struggling**. Kassi is doing great again, and we enjoyed an amazing five-mile hike together just this week. She would have never been able to do that when she weighed 300 pounds, and I am happy to have my healthy, active friend back.

MY BUTT HURTS, AND I'M COLD

These are common annoyances as you lose a significant portion of subcutaneous fat. Fat or adipose tissue is an insulator for our bodies. It also cushions and protects our bones and vital organs.

Being uncomfortable sitting on hard chairs and feeling cold are trials you will learn to navigate. Arrive early to get the soft chairs or bring a cushion. Many patients wear an extra layer or insulated clothing until their body adjusts to cold weather. One of the most excellent tools on your bariatric journey is to

plan ahead. Start practicing now with your food choices, activity, healthcare, and comfort. You do it for the ones you love—do it for yourself as well.

NO MORE DIABETES; NO MORE HIGH BLOOD PRESSURE!

Improvements in type 2 diabetes and hypertension are two of the most remarkable effects of metabolic bariatric surgery (the sleeve and bypass) that too few are aware of, even in healthcare.[39] Research is ongoing to understand the exact mechanisms for these benefits. I have only met one patient who did not end up in remission for diabetes after surgery. Most patients with high blood pressure are off at least one of their medications before they go home from the hospital, and many never need blood pressure or diabetic medication again.[40]

I realize the gravity of these statements. So why aren't these effects more talked about? I still have patients come for follow-up visits and talk about how amazed their primary care doctor is that they no longer need medication for diabetes or high blood pressure. Maybe there is a gap in medical education because we are still learning how this happens. Regardless, it does, and it's incredible.

Stopping medications is among the top reasons patients pursue weight loss surgery. In this country, it seems we take one drug for one problem, then two pills for the side effects of the first drug, and so on. People are tired of spending so much time and money on handfuls of pills. **Fewer health problems and fewer pills** are two of the most significant benefits of bariatric surgery.

Now, if you are still reading, and some of these statements didn't cause you to run in the opposite direction (it's okay if they did!), I hope you will use these insights. Plan ahead and learn more about what you can do before surgery for a smooth journey. Some patients claim going through weight loss surgery was NOT hard. But I guarantee you, those are the ones who worked tirelessly to develop the habits and prepare before surgery.

In the final section, Empowerment, I would like to leave you feeling hopeful and ready to put your new knowledge to use. After all, it doesn't do you any good if it doesn't compel you toward action and changing your current lifestyle. Don't be afraid to reach for the stars—the possibilities could be more than you can imagine!

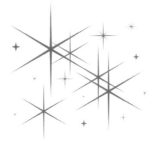

Part 5: EMPOWERMENT

Often, when patients come to us considering weight loss surgery, they feel defeated. No matter how hard they have tried, they cannot lose the weight and keep it off. Remember, the goal is **progress, not perfection**. The beautiful thing is that you have tried! You didn't end up considering weight loss surgery by doing nothing. You are thoughtfully moving forward with new knowledge; you have learned from your mistakes and will continue to learn. You are taking action.

Admitting that we need help and asking for it can be pretty challenging. It requires us to acknowledge our limitations and vulnerabilities, which can be uncomfortable. Society often emphasizes self-reliance and independence, making it even harder to reach out for assistance.

Surely, the human race would not have survived and thrived as it has if we had not bonded together as families and communities with common goals. It takes courage to recognize when we need support and to take the necessary steps to seek it. By reaching out for help, we open ourselves up to new perspectives, knowledge, and growth opportunities. So, let's embrace the power of asking for help and unlock your potential for personal development.

With social media as a constant influence and distraction, we have a world of support, ideas, and shareability at our fingertips. As you follow others' journeys and possibly share your own, be sure that you take the opportunity to enlighten those in your circles who don't yet understand what a bariatric path consists of. You can educate through your experience, leading to enhanced support from those around you. They will appreciate all you are doing to succeed. In turn, you can help others by possibly empowering someone as a future support person.

Chapter 14

Focus on the Outcome

> Whatever your mind can conceive and believe, it can achieve.
> — Napoleon Hill

In life, we find ourselves facing an array of choices and challenges. One key principle can **guide us through the maze of decisions and obstacles**:

focus on the outcome.

THE BEACON

Imagine you're setting sail on a vast ocean. Your destination is a distant island, yet you don't know the island's name, its size, what it looks like, or even its direction. You have no idea if it's a huge, jagged rock with towering cliffs or a tropical paradise with smooth white sands, palm trees, and cascading waterfalls. Without a clear idea of where you're heading, your voyage becomes a meaningless drift. Similarly, in our pursuits, having a clear outcome in mind acts as our North Star to help us navigate.

When we set specific goals, we give ourselves a beacon of clarity. Instead of wandering aimlessly, we have a purpose, a direction, and a destination to reach. This clarity not only enhances our motivation but also sharpens our decision-making process.

WE GET WHAT WE FOCUS ON

As previously discussed, when we have a clear understanding of our destination, we can move toward it. If we concentrate on the problem, we will probably get more of it because negative thoughts influence our emotions and behaviors. When we focus on the solution or the desired outcome, we take steps to achieve it.

I remember when I was learning how to drive. I was terrified of the eighteen-wheelers coming at me in the opposite lane. I would fixate on them in fear until my dad pointed out that I was actually veering toward them as they approached in the opposite lane. Scary! Once he taught me to focus on the road in front of me, my lane, and not look at the big trucks, I was fine. I know you're now rolling your eyes and thinking how silly teenagers can be. Thank heaven for level-headed, patient dads!

CREATE A COMPELLING VISION

A compelling vision is a powerful tool for personal growth and success. It starts with the **new story and self-talk that you created** to begin your transformation. Reviewing and applying those will paint an image and vision of your improved life. Allow yourself to dream big and think beyond your current circumstances.

A compelling vision is a clear and vivid picture of what you want to achieve, encompassing your goals, values, and passions. It serves as a guiding light, providing focus and motivation on your journey. Defining your vision can help you align your actions with your ultimate purpose. Such clarity will make it easier to overcome challenges and stay committed to your path. Remember, your transformation is unique to you—don't be afraid to boldly create a vision that excites and inspires you!

OVERCOME DISTRACTIONS

It is through facing and conquering challenges that we discover our true potential and develop resilience. When we encounter obstacles, we must approach them with a positive mindset and a determination to find solutions.

When we **reframe obstacles or distractions as opportunities for learning and growth**, we can shift our perspective and find creative ways to overcome them. Every obstacle is a stepping stone toward success. Embrace the challenges, stay focused on your goals, and believe in your ability.

Seek support from friends, family, and mentors who can offer guidance and encouragement. Remember that many great achievements have been born from the desire to conquer adversity. You will emerge stronger and more capable.

TAKE BACK CONTROL

I'm going to put it bluntly. Don't be a product of someone else's environment. Just because everyone else indulges in Donut Friday doesn't mean you have to. Just because people around you are miserable and feel like crap, it doesn't mean you have to. Be bold and stand out! You will be surprised how your healthy changes inspire others to do the same. As a result, they may become part of your support system.

Be a leader, not a follower. Stay optimistic and keep taking action. Remember, small choices add up to create our current situation. As Tony Robbins says,

"The little things aren't little—they're everything!"

As you continue to take steps in the right direction, you can use the resources in the next section coupled with your bariatric surgeon's guidelines. **You DO deserve to feel good physically and emotionally.**

***

As someone who started uninformed, it has become my mission to learn how to help others on *their* terms, not mine. As a nurse, it is my job to care, first and foremost. I care. We, as bariatric medicine practitioners, care. And so many others care. Now it is your turn. Care for yourself. Give yourself permission to grow and transform perfectly imperfectly. Be brave, work hard, and believe in yourself. The incredible rest of your life awaits. There is no reason why it can't be everything you want it to be.

I would like to end in the next and final chapter with a recurring theme that you may have noticed throughout this book. That is the importance of focusing on our progress without unrealistic expectations of perfection. Sometimes, we are so hard on ourselves that the stress of what we're trying to do can take us backward and make us miserable. You deserve to feel happy and good about yourself. You deserve the life you desire.

Chapter 15

Progress Equals Happiness

The key to happiness is progress. Progress equals happiness.
— Tony Robbins

Isn't it true that we feel better about ourselves and have more joy when we concentrate on being productive, learning, growing, and helping others? Isn't that why we're all here?

Progress and personal growth are essential for a fulfilling and happy life. Still, sometimes, we confuse progress with perfection and place impossible standards on ourselves. Rather than unrealistic ideals, focus on making and acknowledging your progress. It's almost like a form of practicing gratitude because it keeps us optimistic.

DON'T STACK THE DAYS

Some great advice I received a few years ago from *my* behavioral counselor was, "Don't stack the days." I shared this same advice while working with Sharon, a non-surgical patient.

Sharon would come to appointments, shoulders down and looking at the floor. She would step on the scale, see that she lost a half-pound, and start criticizing herself. In my office, she would almost always start by telling me how she "didn't do well last week." I would try to help her focus on her progress, and the conversation often looked like this:

"Sharon, did you lose weight?" I would ask.

"Yes."

"Did you make better choices than you would have before starting this journey?"

"Yes."

"How do you feel?"

"I feel better than I did before I started, and I have more energy."

"Then you are making progress!" I would proclaim. "You are doing what you set out to do. Just keep making those small decisions that add up, taking you in the right direction."

Just because we skipped exercise or had a piece of cake at a birthday party does not mean we failed. Just because we have a day or a few days where things didn't go well doesn't mean we are failing.

Stay centered on your progress.

If you stack the days or weeks and label them or how you're doing as "badly" or "failing," it is likely to lead you to more of that outcome. Often, we don't even realize we're doing it, but we have to quit telling ourselves we're failing. You will have days where things do not go according to plans. That is normal, right? Brush it off, and **keep going**. Please don't get discouraged.

In the pioneering self-help book *Psycho Cybernetics*, Dr. Maxwell Maltz shares his research on our "internal success mechanism." Like a self-guided missile or torpedo pursuing a target, a series of course corrections will take us where we need to go. The torpedo does not travel a straight line directly to its target. It zig-zags back and forth, responding to the feedback it gains when it goes in the wrong direction. Every time we get off course, we can simply **learn from our mistakes and reroute to keep moving toward our target** and desired outcome.

CELEBRATE THE SMALL WINS

It's not supposed to be easy. But, the more you keep trying and the more you keep doing the little things that add up, like taking the stairs and only eating half of the cookie instead of the whole thing, the easier it will get. And you will feel better! Celebrate the small wins. Recognizing your progress, no matter how seemingly insignificant, can boost your motivation and help you keep a positive mindset.

Don't forget about the NSVs (non-scale victories)! Every time you notice that it's easier to do something or your doctor tells you your blood work is improving, you should write it down and celebrate. I remember a sweet lady who got emotional as she told me she went on a date with her husband and slid easily into the restaurant booth for the first time in a long time. That was a great non-scale victory.

Throughout your journey,

celebrate with non-food rewards—get a pedicure or buy that pair of shoes you've wanted. Take the kids or grandkids to a fun, new park or plan a trip. You deserve to celebrate your progress.

MINDSET

Your mindset can completely change things, as the following story demonstrates.

In the Fall of 2022, we lived in Washington State and the kids had just returned to school. We were bombarded with illness after illness, and my five-year-old had high fevers with most of them.

We were still dealing with the COVID pandemic, and local pharmacies were out of children's liquid fever medications. I had run out of the good flavors and only had bubble gum (which they hated) flavored acetaminophen for backup.

Desperate to get my little one to take some medication, I renamed the flavor. I brought her a dose in the little medicine cup, and when she asked me what kind it was with her sad, sick voice, I responded cheerfully, "Party in a cup."

She looked at me surprised, as this was a new flavor, then said pathetically, "Okay." She sipped the medicine and replied, "Mmm, I like party in a cup."

I still give my kids bubble gum medication when they have a fever, and I still call it party in a cup. They ask for the flavor! It's good that I keep the bottles out of reach where they can't read them.

My point in sharing this story is if changing our perception of something can take something disliked and turn it into something desired, why can't we do this with some of the healthy behaviors we may struggle with, like food choices or being more active?

Get creative and change those behavior mindsets from nasty bubble gum to party in a cup!

YOUR DIVINE RIGHT

You are ready! We have built a solid foundation to help you move in the right direction. However, I don't want to leave you with any misunderstanding. So please know that as great as it can be, I'm not saying that weight loss surgery is *the* solution or that it's right for everyone.

My message is that you deserve to **live your best life with vitality**—and without judgment based on your appearance or decisions about your health.

Remember, it's not this book, self-help seminars and courses, mentors, or coaches that empower you. The power to do it all is within you. It is our divine right to grow and progress. Those things help, but **you have the ability** to become the best version of yourself. It's time to let go of everything holding you back—fear, judgment, pain.

What matters is right now. Right now is all we have, so forget about the past. What do you want to do today to progress? Embrace the challenges that inevitably will arise and **step out of your comfort zone** to overcome them.

I sincerely hope you will finish this book feeling determined, worthy, and unstoppable. **I know you can do this**.

Bariatric surgery can be a life-changing tool when coupled with behavior change, but regardless of whether you have weight loss surgery—remember your "why" and how incredible it feels to move toward what's important to you.

Keep your self-talk and the stories you tell yourself positive as you take action to create progress and change. I can't tell you how much joy it gives me and fellow team members to witness your transformations.

When patients walk into the office with newfound health, energy, confidence, and quality of life, they literally light up the room. You have that light within you; don't let anyone make you feel otherwise.

Drop a bombshell on the negative thoughts and judgments—blow them up, and do what you know is right for you. As you stay true to your path and enjoy the benefits of your efforts, you will radiate with purpose and vitality!

RESOURCES

The following resources are included to help summarize steps, provide you with an action plan, and further guide you—I've included several of my quick guides that patients and healthcare providers commonly ask me for. I hope they are useful to you!

Six Steps for Lasting Behavior Change
Family-Friendly Habits to Start Now
Your Bombshell Action Plan
What to Say When You Call Your Insurance Company
The Bariatric Pantry & Refrigerator
Meal & Snack Ideas
Family-Friendly Recipes & How to Modify Your Own
Holiday & Dining Out Tips
Evidence-Based Diet Plans for Healthy Eating Ideas
Your Anytime, Anywhere Guide to Being Active
Recommended Reading

Six Steps for Lasting Behavior Change

1. Find your "why" and rewrite your story

2. Create awareness of your patterns and triggers

3. Become more mindful

4. Self-monitor and plan ahead

5. Build an action plan with goals, support, and accountability

6. Practice flexibility, patience, consistency, and repeat as needed!

Family-Friendly Habits to Start Now

Eat small, frequent meals
Practice eating a variety of proteins
Use a fitness tracker
Carry a water bottle as a reminder to drink water often
Take a multivitamin
Enjoy strengthening, cardiovascular, and stretching activities regularly
Get out in nature for regular sunlight and fresh air
Practice deep breathing and mindfulness
Get adequate sleep
Use guided meditations for stress, sleep, focus, anxiety, and self-awareness
Dine out less
Eat slowly and chew well
Walk and move your body more
Avoid sugary drinks
Plan ahead for healthy choices
Focus on the outcome
Stay centered on your progress
Celebrate with non-food rewards

Your Bombshell Action Plan

> Let your learning lead to action, and you'll create an extraordinary life.
>
> — Jim Rohn

1. What is my why? (From page 68, Finding Your Why exercise)

2. What is the specific result that I am committed to?

Additionally, circle all that apply:

a. Fewer medications
b. Decrease hemoglobin A1c
c. Decrease blood pressure levels
d. Decrease cholesterol levels
e. Increase energy
f. Decrease pain
g. Improve mood

YOUR BOMBSHELL ACTION PLAN

h. Improve functionality (easier to do things) and quality of life

i. Be an awesome support person to my loved one having (or who already had) weight loss surgery

3. What is the story or self-talk language I will use to stay focused regarding the result I desire? (From page 74, My Story in Creating Your Success Mindset)

4. How will I accomplish this?

a. Weight loss surgery (where):

b. Non-surgical route (lifestyle changes and possible evidence-based diet plan):

5. What information do I need in order to accomplish this?

BARIATRIC BOMBSHELL

a. How will I pay?

b. How will I get started?

c. What are the lifestyle changes I will make?

6. What are the behavior patterns I need to change to be successful?

7. How will I interrupt them, or what will I replace them with?

8. How will I practice more mindfulness regarding my eating habits?

9. What can I start doing to plan ahead for better food choices?

10. Which methods will I use to self-monitor?

Circle all that apply:

  a. Tracking app or website (food choices and portions, protein, hydration, activity, stress/mindfulness, sleep)
  b. Paper logs (food choices and portions, protein, hydration, mood, activity, sleep)
  c. Photos
  d. Weight
  e. BMI
  f. Body circumferences
  g. NSVs (how my clothes fit, being able to do things I couldn't, etc.)

11. What are some specific non-scale victories (NSVs) that I would like to accomplish?

YOUR BOMBSHELL ACTION PLAN

12. Who will be my support system?

13. How will I stay accountable?

a. Support group (name or names):

b. Mentor/support person (name or names):

c. Doctor's appointments (surgeon, PCP, specialists' names):

d. Self-monitoring (how I will track):

e. Teach and encourage those closest to me to make changes with me! (names):

14. When will I start my surgical or non-surgical weight loss journey? (goal date):

15. I will **come back to my "why"** and **my story**. I will **stay flexible** and **patient**, and **repeat new behaviors consistently** for a successful outcome and lifelong healthy habits!!!

What to Say When Calling Your Insurance Company

→ You may be able to find coverage information on your insurance company's app or website (without calling). Ensure that you are signed in to your specific policy.

1. Call the "member services" line.
2. Select "benefits" from the automated system.
3. Follow the prompts to select "surgical" or "other benefits."
4. Once you are speaking with a person, ask them, "Do I have coverage for weight loss surgery?"
5. If they ask you for a **CPT code**, the **sleeve is 43775**, the **bypass is 43644 or 43645**. These are the laparoscopic (minimally invasive) procedures.
6. If they respond that one or both of the procedures are a covered benefit, ask them, "**What are the requirements I must meet to qualify for coverage?**"
7. They will probably list several things or refer you to their website. Ask them, "**Will you please send me the requirements in writing?**" (either to your email or physical mailing address). Ask for the name and direct line (phone number) where you can reach the person you are speaking with for future reference.
8. Bring the requirements to your bariatric team.
9. If you are told that you do not have coverage or that weight loss surgery is not a covered benefit (excluded), try again. —Log in to your policy online and check your benefits. Call again and speak to a different person. Check with your human resources (HR) department to find out if they offer an alternative policy that does provide coverage for bariatric surgery.

The Bariatric Pantry & Refrigerator

→ These are just suggestions. Please add or remove items from this list based on your special diet needs and preferences.

→ Remember that dry, tough meats and fruits or vegetables that have strings, seeds, peels, or membranes may bother your stomach for some time after surgery.

Soups and Canned Goods
Olives
Soups (lentil, minestrone, black bean, chicken/beef and vegetable, or other low-fat soups that have a good source of protein)
Beef or vegetarian chili
Low-sodium green beans, corn, artichoke hearts, asparagus, roasted red peppers, other vegetables of choice
Green chiles
Salsa
Light coconut milk
Evaporated low-fat or skim milk
Canned tomatoes, sauce, and paste
Low-fat cream of chicken and cream of mushroom soup
Broth, beef, chicken, and/or bone
Light or no sugar added fruit

Packaged Foods
Whole grain breads, flours, tortillas, pasta
Almond flour
Brown rice

BARIATRIC BOMBSHELL

Ancient grains or ancient grain products (quinoa, amaranth, millet, farro, barley, teff, etc.)
Sprouted grain products
Kodiak Cakes Power Cakes buttermilk mix
Whole grain crackers like Triscuit or Wheat Thins
Oats, whole or steel-cut
Protein powder and/or premade shakes
Meal replacement powder and/or premade shakes
Protein bars (at least 8 grams of protein, low-sugar—less than 10 grams is a good guideline)
Meat alternatives, tofu, tempeh, Beyond Burgers, Morningstar products, veggie burgers, etc.
Soy, almond, cashew, oat, or rice milk (unsweetened)
Maple syrup, sugar-free or 100% pure

Beverages
Gatorade Zero or Gatorade Zero Protein
Powerade Zero
Body Armor Lyte
Diet juice
Crystal Light or other non-carbonated, sugar-free, caffeine-free drinks
Protein water
Herbal tea
Sugar-free hot cocoa mix

Sauces, Dressings, Condiments, and Spreads
Balsamic vinegar
Apple cider vinegar
Red wine vinegar
BBQ sauce, low-sugar or sugar-free
Ketchup, sugar-free
Light or fat-free salad dressings
Low-sodium soy sauce
Sugar-free syrups
Mayonnaise or Miracle Whip, light
Pasta sauce (watch out for added sugar and fat)
Pickles, dill or Splenda-sweetened
Salsa (fresh is best)

THE BARIATRIC PANTRY & REFRIGERATOR

Salad spritzer spray dressings
Sugar-free or natural jam/jelly
Mustards, yellow, spicy brown, whole-seed

Cereals*
Special K protein cereal
Whole or steel cut oats (cook with milk for increased protein)
Cream of Wheat
Kashi Go Lean Crunch
Kashi Peanut Butter Crunch
Unfrosted Shredded Wheat or Kashi whole wheat biscuits
Premier Protein mixed berry almond cereal
Low-sugar granola
*Add ⅓ scoop vanilla protein powder to your milk for increased protein.
*Avoid sugary cereals (10 grams of sugar or more per serving)!

Meat & Seafood* (proteins)
Canned tuna or chicken in water
Tuna and salmon pouches
Sliced deli turkey (nitrate-free)
Extra-lean sliced deli ham (nitrate-free)
Extra-lean ground beef
Extra-lean cuts of beef (eye of round, round tip, top round, bottom round, top sirloin, top loin, chuck roasts—avoid marbling)
Pork tenderloin, loin chops, or sirloin
Chicken breast, skinless, boneless
Ground chicken or turkey breast
Turkey or chicken tenderloins
Turkey burger patties, fresh or frozen
Salmon filets, fresh or frozen
Scallops, fresh or frozen
Shrimp, fresh or frozen
White fish—halibut, cod, tilapia, etc. (wild caught), fresh or frozen, unbreaded
Crab, lump crab (watch out for extra carbs in imitation crab)
Lobster
*Limit your intake of red meats and processed meats like bacon, sausage, hot dogs, deli meat.

BARIATRIC BOMBSHELL

Vegetables
Spring mix salad greens
Microgreens or sprouts
Asparagus
Brussel sprouts
Cabbage
Broccoli
Cauliflower
Baby Spinach
Beets
Bell peppers
Celery
Cucumber
Carrots
Frozen vegetables: green beans, broccoli, mixed vegetables, peas, Brussel sprouts
Lettuce
Garlic
Onions
Scallions
Tomatoes
Zucchini, yellow squash, spaghetti squash

Starchy Vegetables* (high-carbohydrate)
Butternut squash, acorn squash, pumpkin, banana squash
Potatoes
Yams, sweet potatoes (lower in carbohydrate than potatoes)
Corn
*Use small portions, but many of these offer tons of nutrition! Carbs are not your enemy—too many carbs are! —And/or the wrong kind: white or refined flour, bread, crackers, chips, pasta, white rice, fried potatoes, sugary cereals, candy, cookies, cakes, and pastries.

Nuts & Seeds* (healthy fats)
Almonds
Pecans
Walnuts
Macadamia

THE BARIATRIC PANTRY & REFRIGERATOR

Hazelnuts (these 5 are the highest in healthy fats)
Pistachios
Cashews
Sesame seeds, sesame butter, or tahini
Sunflower seeds, raw, shelled
Pumpkin seeds, raw, shelled
Nut butter (peanut, almond, etc.)
Dehydrated peanut butter (PB2, PB Fit—you can eat more because there is less fat)
Sunflower seeds or butter
—I like to make my own trail mix using raw, unsalted nuts and seeds for optimal nutrition.
*Many nuts and seeds have protein in them but are mostly fat; keep portions small at 1-2 tablespoons.
*Peanuts are actually legumes and have more fat than protein in them.

Oils* (healthy fats)
Extra virgin olive oil (best for cooking)
Avocado oil
Flaxseed oil
Sesame oil
Sunflower oil
*Coconut oil is not included due to its high saturated fat content and ability to raise cholesterol levels; canola oil is also controversial due to the way it is processed, along with corn, soybean, and palm oil.[41]
*I recommend avoiding fried foods due to the possible negative health effects.
*You can purchase an oil pump sprayer (pour the oil in and pump it to pressurize it) to use less oil and for even coverage.

Beans & Legumes (good protein sources but often more carb than protein)
Beans (black, pinto, navy, kidney, etc.), canned or dried
Lentils, canned or dried
Peas, dried, canned, or frozen
Chickpeas or garbanzo beans, canned or dried
Soybeans or soybean products; edamame (low-sodium), fresh or frozen

Fruits* (carbohydrates)
Apples
Blueberries, strawberries, raspberries, blackberries,

Frozen fruit with no added sugar (berries are great to keep on hand for smoothies)
Oranges or clementines
Bananas (no more than ½ at a time due to high sugar content)
Grapefruit (avoid with certain medications—check with your pharmacy)
Pears
Peaches
Nectarines
Plums
Prunes (good for fiber)
Unsweetened canned peaches
Unsweetened canned pears
Unsweetened canned pineapple
Unsweetened canned mandarin oranges
Unsweetened canned fruit cocktail
Melons
Grapes
Pineapple, mango, papaya, other tropical fruits (use in moderation due to high sugar content)
*Avoid dried fruits for the most part—they usually have added sugar and are hard for your stomach to break down.
*I recommend berries as a low-carbohydrate, high-fiber, high-nutrient fruit option!

Dairy and Eggs* (proteins)
Butter or omega fatty acid (healthy plant oils) margarine
Cheese, low-fat (part-skim mozzarella is a good one)
Cottage cheese, low-fat or fat-free
Sour cream, low-fat or fat-free
Laughing Cow Light cheese wedges
Eggs, fresh and hard-boiled
Mozzarella string cheese
Ricotta cheese, part-skim
Milk, 1% or skim
Yogurt, low-fat/low-sugar, Greek yogurt (higher protein)
*Too much saturated fat from dairy products can raise your cholesterol levels.

THE BARIATRIC PANTRY & REFRIGERATOR

Baking Items and Spices
Black pepper
Cayenne
Chili powder
Cumin
Cinnamon
Coriander
Curry
Turmeric
Basil
Thyme
Fennel seed
Sage
Rosemary
Poultry seasoning
Mrs. Dash
Everything bagel seasoning
Salt (use in moderation)
Garlic powder
Nutmeg
Sesame seeds, chia seeds
Poppy seeds
Oregano
Low-sodium taco seasoning
Vanilla, maple, almond extract
Raw sugar or sugar alternative (use in moderation)
Honey
Baking powder
Baking soda
Cornstarch
Unsweetened cocoa
Splenda, Stevia or other non-nutritive sweeteners (use in moderation)

→ Please do not buy products with high-fructose corn syrup or hydrogenated/partially-hydrogenated oils (trans fats). These are two of the worst things we can put in our bodies!

Meal & Snack Ideas

→ Portions are not included because your surgeon and your stomach will guide you on how much to eat and when. Remember, you should have a good source of protein every time you eat. These are just ideas, so please modify them as needed. Fruits are interchangeable, as are grains (or carbohydrates) and non-starchy vegetables.

→ Each grouping of ingredients or individual items is a meal or snack.

BREAKFAST

Whole wheat English muffin, egg, low-fat cheese, berries

Proatmeal
Oatmeal made with milk, nuts, berries, ⅓ scoop protein powder

Kashi Go Lean Crunch or Peanut Butter Crunch, low-fat milk

Other whole grain cereal with added protein, low-fat milk, berries

Low-sugar (less than 10 grams per serving) whole grain cereal, low-fat milk, ⅓ scoop protein powder, berries

French toast
Low-calorie whole grain bread, egg, cinnamon, vanilla, sugar-free syrup

Meal replacement or nutritional shake

Protein shake with ½ banana

Omelet
Egg, low-fat cheese, pepper, mushroom, onion

MEAL & SNACK IDEAS

Greek yogurt with low-sugar granola, berries

Kodiak Cakes pancake or waffle with sugar-free syrup, turkey or chicken sausage

Breakfast Burrito
Small low-carb tortilla, egg, low-fat cheese, beans (optional), veggies

Jimmy Dean Light Breakfast Sandwich

Fried egg, fruit or low-calorie toast with natural or low-sugar jam

Breakfast Scramble
Egg, cheese, ham or choice of meat if desired, potato, veggies, salsa, avocado (¼ to ⅓ at a time)

Low-calorie whole grain bread, almond or peanut butter/peanut butter substitute (PB2, PB Fit), pair with some low-fat milk or protein shake

Steph's breakfast muffin and some fruit (see recipe in Family-Friendly Recipes below)

Smoothie

Greek yogurt or protein powder, frozen berries, low-fat milk, non-nutritive sweetener if needed, and add some greens for extra nutrition!

LUNCH

Sandwich
Whole grain, low-calorie bread or pita
Turkey breast or extra lean deli meat (preferably nitrate-free)
Low-fat cheese
Low-fat mayo or Miracle Whip
Mustard
Pickles, lettuce, tomatoes, etc.

Southwest Wrap
Low-carb tortilla (whole grain if possible)
Low-fat cheese
Chicken breast or alternative lean protein

BARIATRIC BOMBSHELL

Salsa
Beans (optional)
Lettuce

<u>Tuna & Crackers</u>
Tuna (made with low-fat mayo and sugar-free relish) or tuna pouch
Whole grain crackers
—I like to add onion and celery to my tuna for extra flavor, nutrition, and crunch.

<u>Leftovers</u>
Brown rice or other whole grain
Chicken breast or other protein
Broccoli or other green vegetable

<u>Caesar Wrap</u>
Low-carb tortilla
Chicken breast
Low-fat Caesar dressing
Shredded parmesan cheese
Romaine lettuce

<u>Protein Bowl</u>
Beans or legumes
Quinoa or other whole grain
Lean meat or soy alternative if desired
Mixed greens or baby spinach
Bell peppers, cucumber, onions, and other veggies
2 teaspoons of olive oil
Lemon juice, apple cider vinegar, or flavored vinegar
—You can substitute the olive oil and lemon juice or vinegar for a fat-free or low-fat dressing.

<u>Egg Salad Sandwich</u>
Whole-grain, low-calorie bread
Hard-boiled eggs, low-fat mayo, seasoning
Baby spinach

Lean Cuisine, Amy's, or alternative low-carb, low-fat frozen meal with at least 10 grams of protein

MEAL & SNACK IDEAS

→ Lunch is a better time to eat pasta or potatoes, rather than dinnertime. Also, you can always make sandwiches open-faced. You don't have to try to eat two pieces of bread. You may also substitute bread for a tortilla, pita, or sandwich thin (whole grain).

DINNER

Brown, basmati, or wild rice
Chicken, grilled, seasoned
Green beans

Whole grain pasta or other grain
Salmon fillet, sliced lemon
Salad with fat-free dressing

Open-faced barbeque chicken sandwich
Chicken, cooked, shredded
Sugar-free BBQ sauce
Whole wheat bun (½)
Mixed green salad with low-fat or fat-free dressing

Sweet potato or yam
Sirloin steak
Asparagus

Soft Taco
Low-carb tortilla, small
Chicken breast, seasoned, shredded
Low-fat mozzarella cheese
Lettuce, tomato, onion, salsa
Nonfat sour cream
Black beans (optional)

Brown rice
Chicken breast, seasoned
Green veggies, bell peppers, mushrooms, onions
Olive oil (spray for cooking)

BARIATRIC BOMBSHELL

Pinto beans, cooked
Tomato
Basil
Halibut, sliced lemon
Lemon pepper

<u>Open-faced Sloppy Joe</u>
Extra-lean ground beef
Sloppy Joe mix or make your own
Whole grain bun
Mixed green salad with low-fat or fat-free dressing

Meal replacement shake

Yukon gold potato
Chicken breast
Fresh salsa, cilantro (optional)
Cooked broccoli, green beans, or Brussel sprouts

<u>Personal Pizza</u> (see recipe in Family-Friendly Recipes below)
Whole wheat pita or tortilla, low-carb
Spaghetti sauce
Shredded mozarella cheese
Chicken breast
Vegetables of choice

Yams
Lean, white fish like tilapia, cod, or halibut
Broccoli, green beans, or Brussel sprouts

<u>Salad with Chicken</u>
Romaine Lettuce
Chicken Breast
Balsamic vinegar or fat-free dressing
Fresh mixed vegetables of choice

<u>Chili</u> (see recipe in Family-Friendly Recipes below)
Nonfat sour cream
Fresh tomato, diced
Small side salad with fat-free dressing

MEAL & SNACK IDEAS

<u>Protein-Style Turkey Burger</u>
Ground turkey patty, cooked and seasoned
Veggies of choice (pickle, onion, tomato
Condiments of choice
Green leaf or butter lettuce
—Place patty in lettuce with other ingredients and fold lettuce around burger in place of bun.

Whole wheat pasta
Marinara sauce
Chicken breast or seafood (shrimp, crab, lobster, etc.)
Sautéed vegetables
Olive oil (spray for cooking)

<u>Pot Roast</u>
Lean beef roast, trimmed
Low-sodium onion soup
Carrots, celery, onion, gold or sweet potatoes, mushrooms, green beans, etc.

<u>Tuna Melt</u>
Whole grain low-calorie bread or tortilla
Tuna made with low-fat mayo, sugar-free relish, celery, onion (optional)
Low-fat mozzarella cheese
Baby spinach

SNACKS

Meal replacement or protein shake

Meal or protein bar (low-sugar, 8+ grams of protein)

Apple or other fruit
Natural beef or turkey jerky (no added sugar)

Mozzarella string cheese
Whole grain crackers or fruit

Small smoothie made with Greek yogurt or protein powder and fruit

BARIATRIC BOMBSHELL

Whole wheat pretzels
Natural beef or turkey jerky

Protein chips
Fresh vegetables (carrot, broccoli, cauliflower, cucumber, celery sticks)

Almonds
Fruit

Greek ranch (dip made with low-fat Greek yogurt)
Fresh vegetables

Salsa or fresh tomato
Triscuit
Low-fat cottage cheese
Fresh pepper (optional)

Wheat thins, Triscuit, or other whole grain cracker
Tuna or flavored tuna pouch

Celery sticks filled with PB2 or PB Fit (reconstituted with water)

Whole grain crackers or slice of low-calorie bread
Egg salad

Greek yogurt
Low-sugar granola
Berries

Fruit
1% cottage cheese

Soy nuts

Whole grain crackers or protein chips/crackers
Laughing Cow Light cheese

Edamame

Whole grain crackers
Chicken salad made with light mayo

MEAL & SNACK IDEAS

Fruit
Hard-boiled egg

Swiss cheese or low-fat cheese slice
Turkey breast slice
Dill pickle or bell pepper slice
—Roll ingredients together.

Nachos
Whole grain crackers or chips
Shredded cheese
Shredded chicken
Fresh salsa

Sugar-free Jell-O
Low-fat cottage cheese

Low-sugar omega trail mix

Avocado
Lean deli meat
Whole grain, low-calorie bread or whole grain crackers

Whole grain crackers
Cheese
Lean deli meat

Sugar-free hot cocoa with added chocolate protein powder

AFTER DINNER SNACKS (approximately 100 calories of mostly lean protein)

Low-fat Greek yogurt

Protein shake

String cheese

Deli roll (lean deli meat rolled around a pickle spear, cucumber, or bell pepper slices)

BARIATRIC BOMBSHELL

One egg, hard-boiled, fried, or scrambled (add non-starchy veggies if desired)

Lean meat leftover from dinner

Protein popcorn

Small smoothie with berries, greens, Greek yogurt or protein powder

Edamame

Cottage cheese and berries or sugar-free Jell-O

→ Common pitfall foods: nuts, peanut butter, cheese, processed fatty meats, butter/oils, dips, dressings, sauces/condiments, sugary treats and drinks, avocados, white or refined flour/corn/potato products, fried foods.

→ Even though nuts, avocados, and olive oil are healthy fats, they are still fats. Keep portions small to keep excess calories from undoing all your hard work!

→ My recommended portions per meal or snack to avoid excess fats:

Nuts: ⅛ cup
Peanut, other nut or seed butter: 1 tablespoon
Oils and butter: 1-2 teaspoons
Avocado: ¼ to ⅓ of a fruit
Cheese: 1 ounce

→ You will find countless recipes online and shared in your groups. However, just because someone says it is a bariatric recipe does not mean it's healthy. "Keto" does not mean healthy (excess fat). Keep your diet low-sugar, low-fat, and centered on lean protein with a variety of fruits, vegetables, whole grains, beans, nuts, seeds, legumes, and healthy fats. The goal is quality nutrition!

→ Many bariatric patients struggle to eat enough fiber because they are so focused on protein. Protein first, but don't neglect your vegetable, fruit, whole grain, bean, and legume intake. Talk to your dietician or doctor if you struggle to eat a balanced diet (after you advance to a regular diet) after surgery.

Family-Friendly Recipes & How to Modify Your Own

Bariatric patients, please remember that you will need a higher amount of protein compared to other ingredients on your plate. Please follow your surgeon's guidelines.

HAWAIIAN HAYSTACKS
Brown rice, cooked (1 cup dry)
Chicken breasts, seasoned and shredded (approximately four)
Celery, chopped
Tomato, diced
Green onion, chopped
Low-fat shredded cheese blend of choice
Pineapple tidbits
Shredded coconut
Crispy chow mein noodles (I use La Choy brand)
Low-fat cream of chicken soup (thinned with water for gravy-like consistency)
Cholula or hot sauce of choice if desired
Place ingredients in serving bowls in desired amounts. Build haystacks with rice and chicken on bottom. Add remaining desired ingredients and cream of chicken gravy. Bariatric patients can skip crispy noodles and/or pineapple and coconut to prevent dumping syndrome and excess carbohydrates.

CURRY APPLE CHICKEN

1.5 tablespoons avocado oil
2-4 teaspoons mild yellow curry powder
1 apple, diced
1 onion, diced
4 chicken breasts or approximately 8 chicken tenders
1 small can low-fat cream of mushroom soup
1 ½ cups light coconut milk or low-fat canned milk

Sauté onion, apple, curry powder in oil until onion is tender. Add milk and cream of mushroom soup. Stir until blended. Arrange chicken in 9 x 11 baking dish. Pour sauce over chicken. Bake at 350°F for 25-45 minutes, depending on the thickness of chicken, until it reaches 165°F. Check doneness with a meat thermometer after 25 minutes. Allow to cool slightly before serving with your favorite grain (I like brown rice) and green vegetables (broccoli is delicious with this dish).

GREEK SALAD

Baby spinach or dark leafy greens of choice (not iceberg lettuce)
Protein of choice: chicken breast, extra-lean ham or pork, etc.
Feta and or mozzarella cheese chunks
Bell peppers, chopped
Red onion, chopped
Banana peppers
Cucumber, sliced or chopped
Tomato, diced
Avocado, diced
Greek olives
Lemon juice, olive oil, balsamic or apple cider vinegar (or dressing of choice)
Salt and pepper, if desired

Place ingredients in serving bowls in desired amounts. Build salad according to personal preferences.

FAMILY-FRIENDLY RECIPES & HOW TO MODIFY YOUR...

STEPH'S STREET TACOS
Corn tortillas (small)
Protein of choice (seasoning of preference), extra-lean beef or pork, chicken, grilled fish
Lettuce or cabbage, shredded
Tomato, diced
Onion, chopped
Avocado or homemade guacamole
Shredded low-fat cheese blend of choice
Salsa
Sour cream, low-fat
Shredded cheese, low-fat
Cilantro, chopped
Lime wedges
Radishes, sliced
Chipotle Cholula or hot sauce of choice
Place ingredients in serving bowls in desired amounts. Build tacos according to personal preferences.

BUILD YOUR OWN PIZZA
Whole-grain tortilla (small, low-carb for bariatric patients)
Pizza or marinara sauce
Mozzarella cheese, shredded
Grilled chicken breast, shredded or chopped
Veggies of choice (bell pepper, onion, mushroom, etc.)
Olives (optional)
Make individual pizzas according to personal preferences. It can be helpful to sauté the vegetables to reduce the water content and keep your pizza from getting soggy. Line the lower rack of your oven with tin foil to catch any ingredients that may fall. Bake pizzas on an open rack (for crispy crust) at 250°F for 5-15 minutes. Adjust time and temperature as needed. Allow to cool slightly before eating.

BLACK BEAN CHILI

One 15-ounce (425 g) can pinto beans
One 15-ounce (425 g) can black beans
1 ½ tablespoons extra virgin olive oil
2 green bell peppers, chopped
1 onion, chopped
4 garlic cloves, crushed
½ cup fresh parsley, finely chopped
1 pound extra-lean ground beef, ground turkey, or meat alternative
1-2 tablespoons chili powder
Two 15-ounce (425 g) cans diced tomatoes
Salt and pepper to taste (optional)
1/2 teaspoon cumin (optional)

Sauté green pepper and onions in olive oil until tender. Add garlic and parsley. Sauté for one more minute. Remove from heat. In separate skillet, brown meat or prepare meat alternative. Add to onion and pepper mixture. Stir in chili powder and optional cumin, salt, and pepper. Cook on medium-low heat for five minutes. Combine ingredients and add to large pot or kettle. Simmer for one hour. Serve with dollop of light sour cream or low-fat plain Greek yogurt.

FAMILY-FRIENDLY RECIPES & HOW TO MODIFY YOUR...

GRILLED HAM AND CHEESE WITH SOUP
Whole-grain bread or tortilla
Low-fat colby jack cheese or cheese of choice
Extra-lean deli ham (nitrate-free)
Sesame tahini, spray oil, or butter
Everything bagel seasoning (or seasonings of choice)
Place ham and cheese between two slices of bread or tortillas in desired amounts. Spread thin layer of tahini, spray oil, or butter on outside surface of bread, then sprinkle with everything bagel seasoning or seasonings of choice. Place sandwiches in pre-heated skillet with lid and cook on medium-low heat until bread is toasted brown and cheese is melted. Serve with your favorite soup and a crispy dill pickle spear on the side, if desired.

BEST TACO SALAD EVER
Romaine lettuce, chopped
Tomato, diced
Green onion, diced
Avocado, diced
Black, kidney, or pinto beans (or combination)
Extra-lean ground beef, turkey, or meat alternative (prepared with low-sodium taco seasoning)
Low-fat shredded cheese of choice
Cilantro, chopped (optional)
Lime wedges (optional)
Salsa
Light sour cream
Red wine vinegar, sweetened with stevia or Splenda to taste
Lime tortilla chips, crumble on top of salad (optional)
Hot sauce of choice (optional)
Build salad according to personal preferences. Be careful because you can end up with a mountain of a salad due to all the ingredients. Bariatric patients can skip the crumbled tortilla chips to prevent dumping syndrome and for a healthier version.

BARIATRIC BOMBSHELL

CINNAMON VANILLA FRENCH TOAST
4-6 slices of whole-grain bread, depending on size
3 eggs
¼ cup low-fat milk
1 teaspoon cinnamon
1 teaspoon vanilla
Wisk together ingredients with exception of bread. Saturate bread in mixture. Cook both sides in non-stick pan on medium heat until golden.

BREAKFAST MUFFINS
6 eggs
⅓ cup low-fat milk
⅓ cup plain low-fat Greek yogurt
½ cup Kodiak Cakes Power Cakes buttermilk mix
1 cup of sautéed onion, bell pepper, mushroom or veggies of choice (I sauté a whole pan of veggies and use the leftovers for dinner that night.)
1 cup chopped fresh baby spinach
Fresh tomato, small, diced
Salt and pepper
Fennel seed, basil, and/or other herbs of choice
Sprinkle shredded cheese on top if desired
Beat or wisk together eggs, milk, and Greek yogurt in a large mixing bowl. Mix in Kodiak Cakes mix and add remaining ingredients. Stir for consistency. Spoon into silicone or foil muffin liners (¾ full). Bake at 325°F for 20 minutes or until edges of muffins are golden brown.
Makes 1 dozen muffins. Double the recipe and freeze leftover muffins if desired.

***

FAMILY-FRIENDLY RECIPES & HOW TO MODIFY YOUR...

There's no reason to get rid of your favorite family recipes. Instead, simply modify them to make them healthier:

- Use whole grain pasta, breads, tortillas (first word in ingredients list should be "whole", not "enriched").

- Replace at least ½ of the white flour with whole grain flour in recipes.

- Decrease oil or butter by ¼ to ½.

- Replace half the butter or oil with unsweetened applesauce when baking.

- Decrease sugar by ⅓ when baking. No one will notice with most recipes. Or replace the ⅓ with non-nutritive sweeteners, but check conversion charts for the amount.

- Add low-calorie veggies (mushrooms, bell peppers, onions, celery, cucumber, tomato, carrot) to foods to raise the nutrition content of meals and snacks.

- Add extra protein (eggs, meat, dairy, meat alternatives).

- Decrease carbs or starchy veggies.

- Always include a protein, carb, and low-calorie veggie with dinner for family-friendly meals.

- Bariatric and weight loss patients can skip the carbs with dinner and fill up on protein and veggies.

Holiday & Dining Out Tips

Holidays, birthdays, family get-togethers, work events, and social outings can be difficult to navigate. Set a goal now—maintain, don't gain, OR continue to lose weight!

- ★ Find out what will be on the menu ahead of time if you can, and plan ahead.
- ★ Make sure you're hydrated, as thirst can be mistaken for hunger.
- ★ Be sure you're not overly hungry and likely to overeat.
- ★ Ask for a takeout container at the beginning of your meal when dining out.
- ★ Share an entree.
- ★ Ask for sauces and dressing on the side.
- ★ Dip your fork in dressings and sauces rather than pouring it on food.
- ★ Grilled chicken and white fish are low-fat, lower-calorie options.
- ★ Limit alcoholic beverages.
- ★ Bring your own sugar-free, noncarbonated mocktails like diet cranberry juice or non-alcoholic cocktail alternatives—there are MANY to choose from online. I love Moment non-alcoholic botanical drinks.
- ★ Use a smaller plate if possible.
- ★ Practice mindfulness and eat slowly.
- ★ Eat until you are no longer hungry rather than full.
- ★ Snack wisely.
- ★ Encourage friends and family to go for a walk. It will add to the memories you create and help keep your metabolisms healthy!

HOLIDAY & DINING OUT TIPS

→ Some people put an average amount of food on their plate (knowing they can only eat a small amount), enjoy eating small bites slowly, then wrap up the rest and save it for later. This at least takes some of the attention away from a lack of food on your plate.

Remember to enjoy time with loved ones rather than focusing on the food—holidays are about tradition, celebration, and good times with family and friends!

Evidence-Based Diet Plans for Healthy Eating Ideas*

- **DASH** Eating Plan (Dietary Approaches to Stop Hypertension)*
  From the National Institutes of Health.

- **Mediterranean Diet***
  Read about this diet on mayoclinic.org, heart.org, or hopkinsmedicine.org.

- **TLC** (Therapeutic Lifestyle Changes) to Lower Cholesterol*
  From the National Heart, Blood, and Lung Institute.

- **Mayo Clinic Diet***
  This recently changed from a free diet to a paid subscription (starting at $5/month), but it appears to be worth it.

- **Noom***
  An overall great program for healthy lifestyle education, meal and exercise planning, behavior change, and accountability. Paid subscription after free trial.

*Always talk to your doctor before making changes to your diet.
*For bariatric patients, suggestions from these diets are to be used only in adherence to your bariatric surgeon's guidelines.
*There are other diets supported by research, but I have chosen the top-proven and easiest to follow that do not leave out any food groups.

Your Anytime, Anywhere Guide to Being Active

Sweating is self-care.

— My Fitness Pal

→ Always talk to your primary care provider before making changes to your activity level. When a doctor has cleared you and are ready, make gradual increases to your activity level, as tolerated.

→ Please remember to warm up and cool down (starting and stopping exercise abruptly can be hard on your heart).

→ See Acefitness.org or other reliable resources for complete exercise demonstrations and explanations. Please ensure you learn and practice proper form to prevent injury.

→ You can incorporate steps 1-4 into a full-body workout (indoors, outdoors, or in place) or break up activities into small bouts throughout the day.

1. WARM-UP (5-10 minutes every time you are active)

- Walk or march/walk in place and add some arm raises.
- Get the blood flowing to all your major muscle groups
- Bring your heart rate up gradually

2. STRETCH AND LOOSEN UP! (preferably daily)

- Hold stretches for 20 seconds—don't forget to breathe
- Stretching is more effective after your warm-up

3. STRENGTH/RESISTANCE TRAINING (2-4 times per week)

→ 20-30 minutes
→ Do it all at once or break it up into shorter bouts throughout the day
- YOGA
- PILATES
- WORKOUT VIDEO (a good workout video will include your warm-up)
- CALISTHENICS

→ You can find countless options for strengthening on your TV and online (YouTube). Please choose what works for you from a reputable source.

4. CARDIO (work your way up to 30-55 minutes 4-7 times per week)

- Go for a walk, hike, swim, or bike ride
- Use your treadmill, stationary bike, or elliptical
- March or walk in place while watching TV, add arm raises
- Put on a workout video
- Attend a workout class
- Don't forget to take the stairs, park farther away, and get extra steps however you can! Everything counts!!

→ Do some more stretching to prevent stiffness after exercise.

YOUR ANYTIME, ANYWHERE GUIDE TO BEING ACTIVE

The following are my favorite calisthenic exercises for strength. You can do these anytime and almost anywhere. Take a break at work, get out of your chair, and do a set of one or two exercises. Do them at home in between tasks. Stop while you're walking and use a bench or wall to stabilize and complete a set.

Perform repetitions of each exercise to the point of mild discomfort or "burn." That may be seven repetitions, or it may be seventy. Don't stop just because you get to a certain number. For a full-body workout, do 1-3 sets of each exercise. Try doing the floor exercises on your bed if getting on the floor is not an option. Again, don't forget to breathe.

Push-ups

Wall push-ups, table push-ups, bent-knee, or traditional.

Seated bent over rear-shoulder (deltoid) fly

Use cans or light dumbbells for more resistance. Keep your neck straight.

Lunges or squats

Or wall squats if the others bother your knees and/or hips.

Standing Calf Raises

Single-leg calf raises for increased difficulty (hold on to something).

Glute Bridge

Side-leg raises, clams, and/or donkey kicks for an alternative.

Floor Crunches or Plank

Wall plank, leg lifts, or any other abdominal exercise for an alternative.

Contralateral Limb Raises or Alternating Superman

Recommended Reading

Books

- *The Bariatric Bible: Your Essential Companion to Weight Loss Surgery*, Carol Bowen Ball, 2020
- *The Big Book on Bariatric Surgery: Living Your Best Life After Weight Loss Surgery*, Alex Brecher, 2015
- *The Big Book on the Gastric Bypass: Everything You Need to Know to Lose Weight and Live Well with the Roux-En-Y Gastric Bypass Surgery*, Alex Brecher, 2015
- *The Big Book on the Gastric Sleeve: Everything You Need to Know to Lose Weight and Live Well with the Vertical Sleeve Gastrectomy*, Alex Brecher, 2015
- *Filling Up: The Psychology of Eating*, Justine J. Reel, 2016
- *Intuitive Eating*, Evelyn Tribole, 2020
- *The Success Habits of Weight Loss Surgery Patients*, Colleen M. Cook, 2003
- *The Weight Loss Surgery Coping Companion*, Tanie Miller Kabala, 2015
- *Weight Loss Surgery Does Not Treat Food Addiction*, Connie Stapleton, 2017
- *Weight Loss Surgery for Dummies 2nd Edition*, Marina S. Kurian, 2012

RECOMMENDED READING

Websites

- Academy of Nutrition and Dietetics: http://eatright.org
- The American Council on Exercise (ACE): http://acefitness.org/resources/everyone/exercise-library
- The American Society for Metabolic and Bariatric Surgery: http://www.asmbs.org
- Centers for Disease Control and Prevention (CDC): http://www.cdc.gov
- Medical Billing & Coding: http://www.medicalbillingandcoding.org/health-insurance-guide/overview
- My Fitness Pal: http://www.myfitnesspal.com (for tracking and balanced, low-calorie dinner recipes)
- National Institutes of Health (NIH): http://www.nih.gov
- The Obesity Action Coalition (OAC): http://www.obesityaction.org
- The Obesity Society (TOS): http://www.obesity.org
- Tony Robbins: http://www.tonyrobbins.com
- US Department of Health and Human Services: Office of Disease Prevention and Health Promotion: http://www.health.gov

ACKNOWLEDGMENTS

My heartfelt thanks to the following:

Cris C., Jennifer D., Kelsey F., Rebecca F., Wanda G., Kassi H., Dani O., Jon P., Andrea S., Danielle S., and Lisa S. Without you, this book would not exist.

My husband, Dave, and my kids for being patient and supporting Mommy to live her dreams and help more people.

My parents and older brother, Brandon, for instilling in me their passion for healthy and outdoor living and for your love and encouragement. Lindsay Child and Jarom Bunderson for always believing in me and supporting me with enthusiasm!

Ruth Bunderson, loving grandmother and WWII nurse: Your love, strength, and example carry me through, and I miss you every day.

Dr. Justine Reel, my favorite professor: Thank you for so graciously offering your review and all the work you do to help those suffering from disordered eating.

Krikit Butcher and Melissa Oldham: Two exceptionally kind and beautiful women who without, I would not have been able to hold it together in intense work situations and the stress of COVID. Thank you for being true friends and making me laugh.

Special friends, Traci, Kassi, and Amy: I can't imagine life without you, Kass and Trace. Thank you for always being there and letting me be me. Amy, I miss you so much and will never stop fighting to be the woman you believed me to be.

St. George Word of Mouth Facebook group survey participants: Thank you for sharing your thoughts and experiences for this book in order to help future bariatric patients and their loved ones.

To all my remaining friends, family, and patients: Each of you plays a role in my life, experience, and growth, and I am grateful for you.

PERMISSIONS

Dean Graziosi's Mastermind.com team was consulted and permission was granted for the use of Dean Graziosi's "Why You Must Find Your Why" story.

Tony Robbins' team was consulted and confirmed that there are no copyright infringements, and proper acknowledgments have been given regarding the quotes and concepts that have been shared from his media. As a disclaimer, I'm not affiliated with Tony Robbins and haven't spent thousands of dollars on his seminars and coaching. Most of his fundamentals are free. He gladly shares the basics to help us get started, then offers more in-depth guidance for those who desire it.

Kelsey's and Kassi's stories are used with permission.

Dani's and Lisa's comments are shared with permission.

Additionally, direct quotes from privacy-protected patients and healthcare providers have been used with their permission.

NOTES

1. U.S. Department of Health and Human Services. (2023). *Weight-loss (bariatric) surgery - NIDDK*. National Institute of Diabetes and Digestive and Kidney Diseases. https://www.niddk.nih.gov/health-information/weight-management/bariatric-surgery

2. American Society for Metabolic and Bariatric Surgery. (2022). *Estimate of Bariatric Surgery Numbers, 2011-2021*. ASMBS. https://asmbs.org/resources/estimate-of-bariatric-surgery-numbers

3. Boyd, P.J. (2020, March 2). *Gwyneth Paltrow said starring in Shallow Hal was a "disaster"—here's why she is right*. The Guardian. https://www.theguardian.com/film/shortcuts/2020/mar/02/gwyneth-paltrow-said-starring-in-shallow-hal-was-a-disaster-heres-why-she-is-right

4. American Society for Metabolic and Bariatric Surgery. (2021, July). *Metabolic and bariatric surgery*. ASMBS. https://asmbs.org/resources/metabolic-and-bariatric-surgery

5. Johns Hopkins Medicine. (2019, November 19). *Dumping syndrome after gastric bypass surgery*. Hopkins Medicine. https://www.hopkinsmedicine.org/health/wellness-and-prevention/dumping-syndrome-after-gastric-bypass-surgery

6. Ashrafi, D., et al. (2020, March 8). *Bariatric surgery and gastroesophageal reflux disease*. Annals of Translational Medicine. https://www.ncbi.nlm.nih.gov/pmc/articles/PMC7154328/#r17

7. Billeter, A. T., et al. (2014, June 3). *Malabsorption as a therapeutic approach in bariatric surgery*. Viszeralmedizin. https://www.ncbi.nlm.nih.gov/pmc/articles/PMC4513825

8. Kashyap, S. R., et al. (2010, July). *Bariatric surgery for type 2 diabetes: Weighing the impact for obese patients*. Cleveland Clinic journal of medicine. https://www.ncbi.nlm.nih.gov/pmc/articles/PMC3102524

9. Stahl, J. M., et al. (2023, July 24). Obesity surgery indications and contraindications. https://www.ncbi.nlm.nih.gov/books/NBK513285

10. McPhee, J., et al. (2015, November 23). *Suicidal ideation and behaviours among adolescents receiving bariatric surgery: A case-control study.* European eating disorders review : the journal of the Eating Disorders Association. https://www.ncbi.nlm.nih.gov/pmc/articles/PMC4710087

11. Cleveland Clinic. (2022, September 12). *Visceral fat: What it is & how to get rid of it.* https://my.clevelandclinic.org/health/diseases/24147-visceral-fat

12. American Society for Metabolic and Bariatric Surgery. (2023). *Who is a Candidate for Bariatric Surgery?.* ASMBS. https://asmbs.org/patients/who-is-a-candidate-for-bariatric-surgery

13. Sogg, S. et al, (2016). *Recommendations for the presurgical psychosocial evaluation of bariatric patients.* ASMBS. https://asmbs.org/app/uploads/2016/06/2016-Psych-Guidelines-published.pdf

14. American Society for Metabolic and Bariatric Surgery. (2020). *FAQs of bariatric surgery.* ASMBS. https://asmbs.org/patients/faqs-of-bariatric-surgery

15. Telem, D. A., et al. (2017). *American Society for Metabolic and Bariatric Surgery: Care pathway for laparoscopic sleeve gastrectomy.* ASMBS. https://asmbs.org/app/uploads/2017/06/PIIS1550728917300412-1.pdf

16. Graziosi, D. (2021, March 8). *Why you must find your "why."* Dean Graziosi. https://www.deangraziosi.com/why-you-must-find-your-why

17. Robbins Research International, Inc. (2023). *One decision to change your life.* Tony Robbins. https://www.tonyrobbins.com/stories/unleash-the-power/change-your-story

18. Hooker, S. A., et al. (2018, February 28). *Encouraging health behavior change: Eight evidence-based strategies.* American Academy of Family Physicians. https://www.aafp.org/pubs/fpm/issues/2018/0300/p31.html

19. Aronov-Jacoby, S. (2022, January 27). *The benefits of self-awareness.* Humber River Health. https://www.hrh.ca/2022/01/27/the-benefits-of-self-awareness

20. Peterson, N. D., et al. (2014, September). *Dietary self-monitoring and success with weight management.* Obesity (Silver Spring, Md.). https://www.ncbi.nlm.nih.gov/pmc/articles/PMC4149603

21. Burke, L. E., et al. (2011, January). *Self-monitoring in weight loss: A systematic review of the literature*. Journal of the American Dietetic Association. National Center for Biotechnology Information. https://www.ncbi.nlm.nih.gov/pmc/articles/PMC3268700

22. National Institutes of Health. (2023). *Aim for a healthy weight: Key recommendations*. National Heart Lung and Blood Institute. https://www.nhlbi.nih.gov/health/educational/lose_wt/recommen.htm

23. Unites States Department of Agriculture. (2023). *Food and Nutrition Information Center (FNIC) FAQs*. National Agricultural Library. https://www.nal.usda.gov/programs/fnic

24. Keller, U. *Nutritional laboratory markers in malnutrition*. J Clin Med. 2019 May 31;8(6):775. doi: 10.3390/jcm8060775. PMID: 31159248; PMCID: PMC6616535.

25. American Society for Metabolic and Bariatric Surgery. (2021, August 6). *Metabolic and bariatric surgery fact sheet:* ASMBS. https://asmbs.org/resources/metabolic-and-bariatric-surgery

26. Cleveland Clinic. (2023, October 9). *What's a complete protein and should you care?* Cleveland Clinic. https://health.clevelandclinic.org/do-i-need-to-worry-about-eating-complete-proteins

27. Merritt, A. (2019, March 6). *BMR versus RMR*. American Counsel on Exercise. https://www.acefitness.org/fitness-certifications/ace-answers/exam-preparation-blog/616/bmr-versus-rmr

28. Mayo Foundation for Medical Education and Research. (2015). *Keys to success after weight loss surgery*. Mayo Clinic Health System. https://www.mayoclinichealthsystem.org/-/media/local-files/eau-claire/documents/medical-services/bariatric-surgery/bariatric-surgery-life-after-weight-loss.pdf

29. Frey, M. (2022, July 26). *Bioelectrical Impedance Analysis (BIA)*. Verywell Fit. https://www.verywellfit.com/bioelectrical-impedance-analysis-bia-3495551

30. U.S. Department of Health & Human Services. (2018). *Physical Activity Guidelines for Americans 2nd Edition*. https://health.gov/sites/default/files/2019-09/Physical_Activity_Guidelines_2nd_edition_Presentation.pdf

31. Cleveland Clinic. (2022). *Endorphins: What they are and how to boost them*. https://my.clevelandclinic.org/health/body/23040-endorphins

32. Cleveland Clinic. (2023). *You Guessed It: Long term stress can make you gain weight.* https://health.clevelandclinic.org/stress-and-weight-gain

33. Hinckley, G. B. (2001). Choices and Consequences. *Stand a little taller: Counsel and inspiration for each day of the Year* (p. 147). Eagle Gate.

34. Robbins, T. (2023). *The Time of Your Life.* Tony Robbins Breakthrough App. https://www.tonyrobbins.com/breakthrough-app

35. Ilana N Bezerra et al, *Association between eating out of home and body weight, Nutrition Reviews*, Volume 70, Issue 2, 1 February 2012, Pages 65–79.

36. Mayo Foundation for Medical Education and Research. (2022, October 8). *Metabolism and weight loss: How you burn calories.* Mayo Clinic. https://www.mayoclinic.org/healthy-lifestyle/weight-loss/in-depth/metabolism/art-20046508

37. Division of Nutrition, Physical Activity, and Obesity, National Center for Chronic Disease Prevention and Health Promotion. (2023, August 1). *Benefits of Physical Activity.* Centers for Disease Control and Prevention. https://www.cdc.gov/physicalactivity/basics/pa-health/index.htm

38. Michalak, M., et al. (2021, January 12). *Bioactive compounds for skin health: A review.* Nutrients. National Center for Biotechnology Information. https://www.ncbi.nlm.nih.gov/pmc/articles/PMC7827176

39. Arterburn, D. E. (2020, September 1). *Benefits and risks of bariatric surgery in adults: A review.* JAMA. National Center for Biotechnology Information. https://pubmed.ncbi.nlm.nih.gov/32870301

40. Pareek, M. (2019, March 28). *Metabolic surgery for hypertension in patients with obesity.* American Heart Association. https://www.ahajournals.org/doi/full/10.1161/CIRCRESAHA.118.313236

41. Crosby, G. (2018). *Concerns about canola oil.* Harvard School of Public Health. https://www.hsph.harvard.edu/nutritionsource/2015/04/13/ask-the-expert-concerns-about-canola-oil

Made in United States
Troutdale, OR
05/21/2024